Pleas

BRITISH DOLLS
OF THE 1960s

Roddy baby doll

BRITISH DOLLS
OF THE 1960s

SUSAN BREWER

First published in Great Britain in 2009 by
REMEMBER WHEN
an imprint of
Pen & Sword Books Ltd
47 Church Street
Barnsley
South Yorkshire
S70 2AS

ISBN 978 1 84468 056 6

A CIP catalogue record for this book is
available from the British Library.

Typeset in Bembo by
Phoenix Typesetting, Auldgirth, Dumfriesshire

Printed and bound in Thailand by
Kyodo Nation Printing Services Co., Ltd

Pen & Sword Books Ltd incorporates the imprints of Pen & Sword Aviation, Pen &
Sword Maritime, Pen & Sword Military, Wharncliffe Local History, Pen & Sword
Select, Pen & Sword Military Classics, Leo Cooper, Remember When, Seaforth
Publishing and Frontline Publishing.

For a complete list of Pen & Sword titles please contact
PEN & SWORD BOOKS LIMITED
47 Church Street, Barnsley, South Yorkshire, S70 2AS, England
E-mail: enquiries@pen-and-sword.co.uk
Website: www.pen-and-sword.co.uk

Contents

Foreword

The history of dolls goes back to the earliest civilisations, right around the world from Japan to the Americas. Each culture in each era expressed itself

Sally Tuffin

through many mediums, including of course children's dolls which do so relate to the art and fashion of the day. In Victorian Britain mature designers and craftsmen dressed their dolls in layers of cloth and linen to imitate the appearance of themselves and their children who were dressed as mirror images of their parents.

England in the 1960s was no exception. A liberating decade when young people were empowered to influence art and fashion, and so dolls grew ponytails and wore jeans – when we were asked to design clothes for Sindy it was our natural instinct to dress her as we observed young people in the High Street. Sindy and Barbie epitomised the moment and the aspiration of young girls all over the country. Today, television rules and we will look back and see that our dolls were hugely influenced by television characters, be they real or animated.

My first forays into fashion were when, as a very young girl, my mother taught me to sew and I spent hours and hours cutting and stitching scraps of cloth to make clothes – and hats! – for my dolls.

Sally Tuffin

Introduction

Of all the decades I've lived through, the 1960s was the most colourful – both literally and metaphorically. I recall wandering through Carnaby Street where the latest fashions were to be found and eyeing up the trendy boutiques in Oxford Street. I remember, too, buying my first miniskirt, blacking up my eyes like Twiggy, wearing barely-there lipstick and thinking I was the cat's whiskers when I found a Quant-inspired op art PVC coat. Even if it did come from C&A.

It was a fun decade, a time of lime green, citrus yellow, kingfisher blue

Author, toys, (and cat!), 1960s

and fuchsia pink – and flowers. Flowers everywhere, especially daisies with rounded petals, and all of this was reflected in the doll fashions of the time. In Britain, Sindy burst onto the scene, altering the concept of the fashion doll; almost overnight, it seemed, the large sophisticated teen dolls were out of favour, replaced by a 12-inch high upstart in denim jeans. By the late 1960s, many of the play dolls were sporting the shortest possible dresses in zingy patterns and vivid colours. In addition, they had discovered the powers of speech and movement, thanks to batteries and other clever devices.

This is a look at the development of British dolls of the 1960s, and how the manufacturers became ever more inventive as the decade progressed. Unfortunately, it's impossible to show every doll here, so I have chosen some of my favourites, and I hope that, amongst them, you will find some which appeal to you, too.

Susan Brewer

Timeline

1960

The average UK annual salary was £684. The majority of dolls were now made from vinyl.

1961

The 'pill' went on sale in Britain – the beginning of the permissive society! And, coincidentally, in America Barbie was given a boyfriend, Ken.

1962

The Beatles, a pop group from Liverpool, released their first record, *Love Me Do*, going on to change the face of pop music, and, indirectly, youth culture. Chiltern issued their Babykins doll, acclaimed by the Bethnal Green Museum of Childhood.

1963

'The Great Train Robbery' took place – thieves stole over £2m in the biggest ever train theft. Pedigree launched their teen doll Sindy, an instant success and one which would go on to change the face of the British doll scene.

1964

First broadcast of Radio Caroline pirate radio station, located aboard a ship moored in international waters off the Sussex coast – now teens had their own music source. Gotz began manufacturing Sasha dolls for Sasha Morgenthaler.

1965

The tallest building in Britain, the Post Office Tower, was opened. Pedigree introduced Tiny Tears, a revolutionary baby doll who won the 'Girls' Toy of the Year' award for three years in succession.

1966

England won the football World Cup. Twiggy became the face of 1966 and her fashions were copied by millions. Action Man was introduced following the huge success of Barbie and Sindy.

1967

The BBC launched Radio 1, a pop music channel. Teeny Tiny Tears, Tiny Tears' young sister, made her debut. American giant, Mattel, acquired Rosebud.

1968

First decimal coins released, though Britain wasn't to go decimal for another three years. Palitoy introduced the hair-grow doll Goldilocks, a larger version of the successful Tressy.

1969

Astronaut Neil Armstrong became the first man to walk on the moon. The Investiture of Prince Charles took place at Caernarvon. Palitoy issued their mechanical doll 'Tippy Tumbles', voted 'Girls' Toy of the Year'.

Rosebud 'Beatles' vinyl dolls

Chapter 1

Through the Ages

A popular song of the era included the lines 'England swings like a pendulum do', and though maybe not grammatically correct, it summed up the 1960s perfectly – England was the place to be. To be a British teenager in the 1960s made us, we felt, omnipotent. Suddenly, we were at the epicentre of music, fashion, design and the arts. British was best, the Union Jack was a symbol of all that was good and trendy – and we were in the thick of it. But how and why did it happen? And how did it affect our dolls?

**Victorian
wooden dolls**

How Dolls Evolved

Obviously, no one can be certain who made the very first doll. We do know, however, that figurines resembling dolls have been found in many sites across the globe, including ancient Egypt, Rome and Greece. What we don't know is how many of these were intended for children, as many 'dolls' were used in religious ceremonies, or had a sacred purpose.

In most cultures, play for children is as natural as breathing, and as youngsters adore copying their elders, it is more than possible that little girls created 'babies' from whatever materials came to hand. Maybe a bundle of rags, tied with cord to form a head and body, or perhaps a baby-shaped figure woven from corn stalks, or a handful of clay gouged from the riverbank, moulded into a human shape and left to dry in the sun. Fanciful, maybe, but well within the realms of possibility.

Even in more modern times, children − and their parents − had to be inventive. Money was often scarce and parents couldn't always afford food and clothing, let alone toys, for their offspring. Thousands upon thousands of parents used their initiative to make dolls for their daughters, sometimes using cloth to make a traditional rag doll, with an embroidered face and woollen hair. A more inventive mother might incorporate buttons for eyes, pink felt for cheeks and red felt for a mouth. Some might use dried carved apples, mounting them on stick or wire bodies, padding them with cotton wool and cloth and collecting sheep wool for a wig, or they might make a traditional peddler doll, using a walnut so that the face resembled a wrinkled skin.

Often a devoted father, brother or grandfather would whittle a doll from a piece of wood; the more talented carvers would incorporate joints at the doll's elbows and knees to give plenty of movement. In Germany in particular these 'Dutch dolls' or 'Penny Woodens' became part of a thriving industry, and were sold throughout the world, but there were many skilled carvers elsewhere, including Britain.

Wooden Dolls

Dolls began to come into their own during the Seventeenth Century, when childhood started to be accepted as a separate and important phase, and not just a step to adulthood. In the past, children had often been treated as mini adults, dressed in replicas of their mother's heavily brocaded dresses or their father's smart, tight garments. Once it had been accepted that children needed to wear clothes which gave them freedom of movement, and above all, clothes which gave them freedom to play, children became 'fashionable' – and the fashion was to provide playthings. Dolls appeared on the scene, and soon thriving doll industries emerged, as opposed to the earlier trends of dolls carved as a sideline. The early wooden dolls could be large and quite heavy. Often today we refer to early dolls with pupilless dark glass eyes as 'Queen Anne Dolls', and they are very valuable.

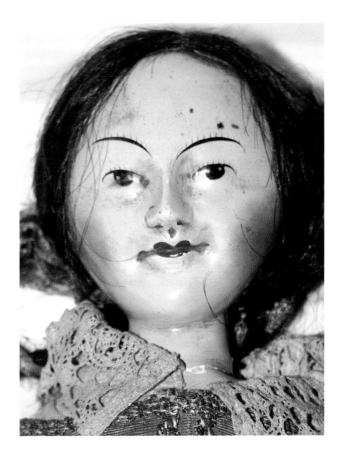

Seventeenth-Century wooden doll

Social historian Henry Mayhew, writing in *The Morning Chronicle* in 1850, found a carver of wooden dolls in London, who said, 'I make the jointed wooden dolls. The turned work (the body) is the work of the turner's lathe. I do it myself, and the faces of the commoner dolls are a composition put on afterwards. I go in for beauty as much as I can, even in the lower-priced dolls. These dolls, now, are carved, after having been turned out of the wood. The carving and drawing – making the eyes, eye-brows, and lips in colours with a fine brush – are the fine touches of the trade. Nice lips and eyes set the article off. The lower-priced dolls have wooden joints at the middle, by which the legs are fastened to the body. We don't go in for symmetry in the commoner sorts of legs; nor, indeed, for any calves at all to them. They are just whitened over. The better ones have nice calves, and flesh-coloured calves too. They are more like nature. The joints of the two sorts are made on the same principles. I buy their ringlets – it's generally ringlets, but, sometimes, braids or plaits, ready made – and have only to fit them on … The arms are stuffed leather, made by others. The best time for my trade was from 1809 to 1816. In every one year that I have named, I made 35 gross of dolls a week, but they were little creatures, some of them 4 inches long, dwarfs of dolls … The little things I spoke of used to fetch a penny, now it's a farthing.'

Papier-Mâché

Papier-mâché was a popular medium for both dolls and puppets, because it was easy to make and to mould, and was also extremely durable. In Sixteenth-Century Britain, travelling actors toured the country, often using puppets to perform plays or tales from the scriptures. Papier-mâché continued to be used for dolls, right up until the early Twentieth Century.

Punch & Judy are the most famous of the early puppets, still with a following today. Punch, who has a long history, was once a marionette known as Punchinello, and was first noted in Britain by Samuel Pepys in his famous diary, where, in an entry for 1662, he wrote 'very pretty the best that I ever saw', after seeing a performance in London's Covent Garden. Another Punch and Judy enthusiast was Charles Dickens, who said, 'In my opinion the Street Punch is one of those extravagant reliefs from the realities of life which would lose its hold upon the people if it were made moral and instructive.'

Wax Dolls

When dolls made from wax appeared, they must have created quite a stir, because the delicate and translucent material resembled the human skin so much, that to little girls of the era they would have seemed real. Additionally, wax felt soft and warm to the touch, and because it could be

Wax doll

poured into a mould it could show the finest features such as tiny noses and shapely lips. By the beginning of the Nineteenth Century, wax was the most popular of the doll-making materials amongst master makers, and although wax dolls did suffer problems with cracking, melting or flaking, it continued to be a well-liked medium right up to the early Twentieth Century.

Wax dolls were shown at the International Exhibition of 1862, where the jury commented that although they respected the lifelike and delicate finish of the dolls, they regretted that it 'diminished the necessity for any effort of imagination on the part of the children who played with them'.

For a while, England was the centre of wax doll-making, with families such as Pierotti and Montanari creating exquisite dolls, often rooting the hair individually into the wax using a hot needle. Many of these dolls were very expensive, affordable by only the richest parents as they were so time-consuming to make, but it wasn't long before cheaper wax dolls appeared. Even if their hair wasn't finely rooted, and the modelling not so skilled, no doubt the dolls were just as equally loved by their young owners.

China Dolls

The turning point was when the first bisque china dolls appeared in quantity. Dolls had been made from china for some time, but at first they tended to be white or highly coloured glossy, heavy examples. They included such dolls as 'Frozen Charlottes', moulded all-in-one and often referred to as 'bathing dolls' as they could be safely immersed in water.

Bisque is a matt-finished china, which bears a resemblance to the human skin. Dolls made from this became very popular during the Nineteenth and early Twentieth Century. Some of the most exquisite, made by French factories including Bru and Jumeau, were extremely costly, and today these dolls are keenly sought by collectors. It wasn't long before Germany, too, was making bisque dolls, and because the Germans were more adapted to industry and mass-marketing, they had the means to produce the dolls in their thousands. Companies such as Simon and Halbig, Kammer and Reinhart, Heubach, Kestner and Armand Marseille made dolls of varying quality, from top of the range types with delicate colouring, lifelike glass

Bisque doll

eyes, tiny teeth, and beautiful wigs and kid leather or composition bodies, to cheaper kinds with imperfections in the paintwork and shapeless cloth or cheap card bodies.

The German dolls continued to flood into Britain until the First World War, when they were temporarily suspended. Japan then seized the opportunity to show us their dolls, which were often made from a coarse quality white bisque china painted after firing. These Japanese dolls continued to be popular, even when the ban on German dolls was lifted after the war.

German dolls, however, went from strength to strength, and in the 1920s the 'My Dream Baby' by Armand Marseille, with its bent-limbed body, was one of the most popular dolls of the time; most small girls preferring it to the old-fashioned 'double-jointed' girl dolls.

Other Materials

Poorer parents who couldn't afford to buy their offspring these beautiful dolls would give carved wooden ones, or those made from cloth. Companies such as the Dean's Rag Book Company sold calico sheets printed with dolls, ready to be cut out, sewn up and stuffed at home, while other concerns dealt in dolls made from paper or card with their clothes printed on paper. Paper dolls are still very popular today, not only with children but with adults who collect modern fashion versions.

Manufacturers experimented with many materials in their quest to find the perfect substance for making dolls. For a while, cloth was exceedingly popular, with exquisite dolls being produced by Dean's, Chad Valley and Norah Wellings. Often these had moulded faces made from stiffened buckram or pressed felt, with glass or painted eyes and mohair wigs. Unfortunately, cloth isn't a particularly durable medium, but even so, cloth dolls are still made in vast quantities today, primarily for toddlers who love the softness and lightness. Some doll designers do still specialise in cloth

Dean's cloth dolls

notably R. John Wright, an American designer whose felt dolls are very expensive and desirable, and are created for adults.

Other materials with which makers experimented included metal, rubber and celluloid. All had drawbacks. Celluloid did prove popular for a while, and some very beautiful dolls were made, but the substance was dangerous as it caught fire so easily, and it was eventually dropped from toy-making. The material which replaced bisque was composition. Composition, a mixture of various things including glue, plaster, sawdust or cloth fragments, was used for doll bodies, as bisque would have proved too costly and too heavy, and soon it was being used for the heads, too. It could be shaped in a mould but didn't need to be fired, so was cheaper to produce. It was also more durable. Dolls made from this material were made until well into the 1950s, although by then, plastics were the in-thing.

Celluloid doll

Plastics

Modern plastics were developed and refined during the Second World War, and when it ended in 1945, toy factories were keen to utilise plastics. Lightweight, robust and colourful, plastics took the industry by storm, and created a stir in the doll world. During the 1950s, thousands of delightful dolls were made from this material (see my book, *British Dolls of the 1950s*).

The 1950s was a golden age of dolls, with companies such as Pedigree, Palitoy, Roddy and Rosebud creating beautiful, well-modelled, well-constructed plastic dolls of all sizes. Towards the end of the decade, there was a further revolution when a new, more pliable form of plastic came onto the market. Today we know it as 'vinyl', and this is the common-place material we still see in dolls today – but back in the late 1950s, it was radical and exciting. It meant that now dolls could be safely bathed, and that their hair could be directly rooted into the head rather than being a glued-on wig. Dolls were becoming even more durable; they were also becoming less expensive to produce.

This last was, perhaps, not necessarily such a good thing, because as dolls became cheaper, they became expendable. Whereas at one time a doll was a treasured toy, cared for and passed down to younger siblings, as dolls became cheaper, children didn't value them so highly. They became mistreated, their hair was cut, they were scribbled over and eventually thrown away with the rubbish. It seems odd but it is often much more difficult to find a mint or near mint 1960s' vinyl doll, certainly from the later years of the decade when prices began to tumble, than it is to find a perfect bisque doll dating from fifty years before.

Vinyl Chiltern teen doll

Amongst the vinyl dolls of the 1960s were some classics which we still remember with affection today – and some of them are still produced. The softer vinyl allowed for smoother modelling and fine detail, while the surge of interest in fashion design led to interesting and appealing outfits appearing on dolls of the era.

Modern Creativity

Today, even though children's dolls can be bought very cheaply, many people enjoy creating their own dolls, using all kinds of strange materials or techniques. Often, these are not intended for children, they are 'designer dolls' made for adult collectors, or created purely for pleasure by the maker. Modern artists might incorporate freestyle embroidery to completely decorate a cloth doll with elaborate patterns, or mould papier-mâché into a doll shape, before dressing it in foil, sequins, costly silks or metal braid. They might experiment with candle wax to create tiny babies, use a modelling clay to produce delicate fairies, or produce woodland beings from natural materials such as twigs, leaves, acorns and pine cones. Some people knit dolls, or crochet them from cotton, while others will buy a plastic doll and decorate it with whatever takes their fancy. Only recently, someone bought a Barbie doll and embedded diamonds into its face!

Nowadays, vinyl is still the favourite medium for play dolls, though the quality can vary from a firm type to a very soft, baby-feel substance. Also, many of today's dolls are anatomically correct, something which would have been frowned upon in the sixties, certainly the earlier part of the decade, even if it was the so-called 'permissive age'.

1960s' 'Boudoir-type' doll, cloth and wire

Chapter 2

England Swings

It is said that if you remember the sixties, you weren't there, and now-adays those years tend to be associated with change, fashion and mass hysteria caused by a group of Liverpool mop-heads known as The

1960s'
Bamforth
postcard

Beatles. But the early years of the decade weren't like that at all.

When the sixties dawned, none of us realised we were on the brink of enormous cultural revolution! The first couple of years differed little from the late fifties. At first the 'swinging sixties' fashion scene wasn't in evidence outside London, and young girls still tended to follow the fashions of their mothers because it was difficult to find clothes designed especially for teens. Popular music tended to be lightweight, candy floss-type songs, sung by solo artists rather than groups, but by 1964 the groups were making their presence felt. A popular postcard of the time featured a little girl saying her prayers, and ending with, 'And please bless Cliff Richard, The Batchelors, The Beatles, Freddie and the Dreamers, The Rolling Stones, Mark Wynter, Billy Fury, Cilla Black, oh, – and Mum, Dad and Fido!'

We used to listen to the music on our 'trannies' – every self-respecting teen had a transistor radio. Mine was a red Hi-Tone, bought for me as a surprise by my Dad. I loved it, and, through the little earpiece, listened to all the tunes of the day. I could quote the chart position of every record in the top twenty, as could most of my school friends. I bought records too, of course – usually 45 rpm singles, though sometimes I might splash out on an EP, (Extended Play), which had two songs on each side, and I played them on my auto-change record player. Also red, it was a Regentone, and I could load ten records on the spindle at once. After the record played, there would be a satisfying 'clunk' as the next one dropped into place.

In the early 1960s, a dance craze spread across the UK, en route from America. It was called the Twist, and, as Chubby Checker, singer of *Let's Twist Again* and *The Twist* explained, you needed to pretend you were drying your back with a towel, while you swivelled your hips and placed your weight forward on one leg! Twist dresses came into fashion – these multicoloured creations were cut straight to the hips, where they flared out in a mass of tiny pleats which swirled as we danced. I believe I bought mine in British Home Stores. They were normally worn with an enormous pendant on a chain, or else a chain belt.

Impact

People born after the 1960s find it difficult to understand how four young lads made such a staggering impact, not only on the music scene but on life in general. Yet they did – John, Paul, George and Ringo, collectively known as The Beatles, introduced a new, alien, raw, unpolished sound in 1962. Within weeks dozens more pop groups were up there alongside them, just as if they had opened the floodgates, while, at the same time, a young designer called Mary Quant was breaking new ground with thrilling, vivid fashions which complemented the fresh, lively sound. Other designers, such as Sally Tuffin and Marion Foale, were creating new ideas, too – later, these designers would also become involved in the doll world. Youth culture was in, and it was all very exciting. The new vibrant atmosphere wasn't only felt in the world of fashion and music; it seemed to be a coming-together of talented people who were bursting with new ideas in all walks of life.

Doll Consequence

The doll world felt the effect, too; not straight away, of course, as the new ideas took time to filter through – but in 1963 Pedigree Toys introduced a fashion teen doll which they called Sindy. This teen doll is still greatly

**Twiggy doll,
Mattel 1960s**

loved today, with countless admirers worldwide, and soon Sindy was joined by more teens, such as Tressy. Other dolls which brightened the playtimes of 1960s' children included Tiny Tears, Dolly Darlings, Tippy Tumbles, Michele, Sasha, Babykins and Action Man.

By the mid-sixties, swinging UK was at its height, and London, especially an area such as Carnaby Street, was the place to be seen. Boutiques filled with music and trendy colourful clothes appeared on every High Street. Skirts grew ever-shorter, thanks to Mary Quant who introduced the mini, while Tuffin and Foale's revolutionary trouser suits were both smart and comfortable. A young, waif-like fashion model, Lesley Hornby, better known as Twiggy, sporting pale lipstick, huge, long-lashed eyes, cropped hair and never-ending legs, featured in magazines and on hoardings and her look was copied throughout the land. Later, dolls were to appear in her likeness, as they did with so many other cult icons of the day – though often as part of a retro movement rather than being issued at the time. Another fashionable look was ultra long hair, preferably blonde, worn with an eye-brushing fringe, à la singer/actress Marianne Faithfull.

An In-Depth Look At A Twiggy Doll

One 1960s' Twiggy doll which does appear from time to time at doll fairs and other outlets was made by the American company Mattel in 1966, and was sold in Britain as well as in America. Though bearing little resemblance to Twiggy herself, it was nevertheless a pretty doll, very much of its time in style, and is really a must-have for anyone intending to collect dolls representative of the 1960s' era.

The head of the Twiggy doll was based on that of Casey, who was one of Barbie's friends, while the body was a Francine body (another friend of Barbie). Although Twiggy and Casey were the same mould, Twiggy can be distinguished by her shorter hair, lack of earrings and by the heavy row of lower lashes.

The Mattel Twiggy doll measures 10¾ inches high, and is jointed at neck, shoulders, waist and hips. She has click bend knees. Twiggy is made from a rubbery feel vinyl, and features blonde hair, painted forward-looking eyes, 'real' eyelashes and a smiling open/closed mouth revealing top teeth and a

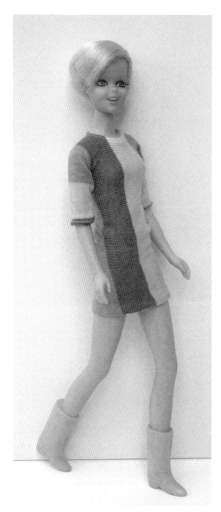

Twiggy doll, Mattel 1960s

tongue. When sold she was dressed in a stretch cotton jersey mini-dress with wide blue, yellow and green stripes. The dress, tagged 'Twiggy Mattel', had three-quarter length sleeves and was teamed with yellow plastic boots. Twiggy came in a pink open-front box printed with the words, 'Here She Is. London's Top Teen Model'. Various costumes were available to buy separately, including 'Twigster', a yellow and orange dress featuring a dazzling geometric design with matching scarf, and 'Twiggy-Dos', a short yellow knitted mini-dress with green stripes. The doll was marked, '1965 Mattel Inc., US Patented. US Pat. Pending. 21 Made in Japan' on her bottom.

At the age of sixteen, Twiggy was named as 'The Face of '66' by the *Daily Express*, and became internationally known – she was the world's first supermodel. Later, Twiggy turned to acting, beginning by starring in Ken Russell's musical *The Boyfriend*, and since 2005 has been linked with the hugely successful advertising campaign for Marks and Spencer. Recently, several other Twiggy dolls have appeared, see Chapter 10.

The Beatles

Without doubt, the major cult icons of the 1960s were The Beatles, who rocketed to fame in 1962 with *Love Me Do*. By 1964 they were pop icons

Beatles vinyl squeezy dolls by Rosebud 1960s

who were mobbed wherever they went. There were outbreaks of mass hysteria at concerts, while tremendous crowds flocked to welcome the boys at airports. Their music was everywhere, as one hit after another soared up the charts – or 'hit parade' as it was known at the time – and Liverpool (The Beatles' home town) was the in-place, suddenly producing many other pop groups, all with the 'Liverpool sound'. The Beatles, though, were at the top, and no-one managed to beat their record sales and song output.

However, dolls of the mop-headed foursome were few and far between. Probably the most well-known are the set made by Remco, which were character-type creations featuring the group with moulded clothing, 'real' hair and overlarge nodding heads. Made from vinyl, each doll came with an autographed guitar (drum kit for Ringo), and were really more ornamental than doll. Woolworths sold Remco dolls at 19/11 the set (just under £1). They also sold Beatles Car Mascots at 14/11 (just under 75p) for a set of the 'Fab Foursome'.

Various sets of 'Beatles' or 'Beatles lookalikes' appeared. Unauthorised and often by unknown manufacturers, though many originated in Hong Kong or Japan, they were usually moulded all in one, with moulded hair and, often, nodding heads, such as a 4-inch high Hong Kong set wearing light grey Beatle suits, and with yellow guitars (white drum for Ringo). Emirober, a Spanish manufacturer, sold plastic bags with John, Paul, George or Ringo header cards, each containing four small plastic figurines pertaining to be the four group members. Each 3-inch high figure was modelled, rather strangely, in self-coloured plastic – red, green, white,

Beatle look-alike by Pelham Puppets 1960s

orange, blue or yellow – and these figures were called 'Beatlemania' on the header card.

British companies were in on the act as well. Rosebud Dolls Ltd. issued a set of four Beatle lookalikes, modelled all in one from soft vinyl, with huge heads and odd-shaped open mouths. Their bodies, arms and legs were all painted black with no attempt to mark on clothing details – in fact the only body detail was a small navel! Each 'Beatle' had a mop of black silky hair, and came with an instrument. These dolls were 7½ inches high, (the heads accounted for 5 inches of that) and were, presumably, intended as toddlers' toys. The Pelham Puppets Company also produced Beatles' clones – in fact, these puppets were probably the most doll-like of all the Beatles dolls. However, to avoid copyright problems they were not referred to as Beatles, and one had a saxophone. Each doll was dressed in a smart round-necked 'Beatle style' grey fabric suit, shirt and tie, had thick black hair and came with a guitar, drums (or saxophone). Other Beatle-type dolls available included the so-called 'gonks' or 'trolls' – polished wooden dolls with oval faces, thick string arms and shocks of black fur 'Beatle hair'. They often carried guitars or a set of drums, and their contemporary styling appealed to trendy 60s' teens (see Chapter 8).

Teens had their own pop music programmes – *Juke Box Jury, Ready, Steady, Go!* and *Thank Your Lucky Stars*. I well remember the tremendous fuss the first time The Rolling Stones appeared; next day, the sole topic of conversation was about the length of their hair. People said they looked like girls. Recently I found a photo of their very first show, and wondered what all the fuss was about. Their hair only just covered their earlobes, but at the time, adults were shocked.

Ready, Steady, Go! was a particularly popular teen television show, featuring all the latest groups and sounds. Presented by Cathy

Cathy McGowan's Boutique

McGowan and Keith Fordyce, it proudly announced, 'The Weekend Starts Here'. In 1967, a kit containing two paper dolls was issued, entitled 'Cathy McGowan's Boutique'. The kit contained boy and girl dolls with lots of paper garments to cut out for them – 'With Fab Gear for Boy and Girl' – and was made by Tower Press. It's very hard to find today with all the outfits still intact.

In 1964, a competition was held to find a name for a new pop music show on the radio. I came up with a name, and to my surprise, it won. The name is still used today, but now by a famous television programme. The name I dreamt up was *Top Gear*, and my prize was a trip to London to spend the day at the BBC with DJ Brian Matthew. I watched from the glass control box as the stars rehearsed and performed their songs – Mark Wynter, Dusty Springfield and The Beatles. It was the height of Beatlemania. The very fact that The Beatles were due to be in the studio was kept top secret, to prevent a crowd of fans forming outside the BBC, so for me to be there, with Paul McCartney making faces at me through the glass, Ringo practising his drumming on a table and John ad-libbing a brilliant impersonation of Mick Jagger, was just amazing.

Other Popular Figures

Many of the 1960s' television programmes and films are today regarded as cult classics, and character dolls were sometimes sold of the actors. However, often the dolls are of a later date, some classic 1960s' figures being issued in the 2000s. Cult programmes/films included *The Avengers*, *James Bond*, *Star Trek*, *Thunderbirds* and *Doctor Who*. The British Fairylite Company issued an Emma Peel doll (the character played by Diana Rigg) from *The Avengers* in 1966. She came complete with three additional outfits, while, two years later, a Japanese company produced a doll purporting to be Tara King. A popular television series of the time was *Dr Kildare*, starring the handsome actor Richard Chamberlain. The Linda Company made a Dr Kildare doll in 1963, dressed in his hospital white top and trousers.

Fairylite also manufactured a series of Thunderbirds dolls in the 1960s, including, of course, Lady Penelope, as well as Scott and the rest of the

Tracys, Brains and Parker. Several other dolls based on television and film characters appeared during the 1960s, including *Mary Poppins* and *Dr Dolittle*, whilst the American Madame Alexander Company issued dolls from *The Sound Of Music*.

Flower Power

Vivid colours, dramatic patterns, long slinky boots, cheeky caps and chunky plastic jewellery were the order of the decade – girls wanted to be noticed, and all aspired to be flat-chested, skinny and with enormous sooty black-surrounded eyes. Of course, all these trends were duly noticed by the doll designers and passed on to their creations – as were the more gentle fashions of the later years of the decade. This was when the hippie movement spread to Britain from America, when both girls and young men bedecked themselves with flowers, beads and tinkling bells. The look involved ethnic designs, looser floaty garments, tie-dyed fabrics and cheesecloth, often crocheted or bearing long fringes, and worn with

Sixties' memorabilia

sheepskin-edged suede jackets. The style continued into the seventies – but by then, the hippie movement had changed, losing the original innocence of the early days.

The sixties wasn't all happiness and sweetness, however; music became increasingly raw, while rival gangs who styled themselves Mods and Rockers battled on beaches, including those at Brighton and Clacton. On the whole, though, it was a fun era – homes featured psychedelic fabrics in swirling pinks, purples and lime, vividly-coloured hand-painted Poole pottery, op art black-and-white patterns, astro lava-lamps with floating globules of coloured wax inside, and weird creatures called glooks with fluffy hair (see Chapter 9). Perhaps the most technical events of the decade were to do with the space missions, culminating in that momentous walk by Neil Armstrong, as he stepped from the Apollo capsule and said, 'That's one small step for man, one giant leap for mankind.' We all gasped as we watched the grainy images on our black and white television sets, staying up till the small hours, gripped with the historical event we were watching.

Sixties' designs were young and crazy, or, in the terms of the day, fab and groovy. Everything was 'swinging'. And it was all reflected in the dolls through their fashions, hairstyles and even make-up – although the more extreme of the sixties' fashions weren't captured doll-wise until the 2000s, when a whole army of fashion dolls aimed to encapsulate the spirit of the sixties (see Chapter 11).

Collecting at the Time

Doll-collecting at this time wasn't something the average adult did. You played with dolls as a child, but by the time you reached the middle years of senior school, they were firmly put aside – although a brave few did dare to keep a Sindy doll or maybe one of the big-eyed Japanese 'boudoir type' dolls to decorate a bedroom.

There was really only one way that a doll-lover could justify a doll collection, and that was if the collection consisted of costume dolls from foreign lands. So that is what we did! Dolls in national or regional costume were very popular in the 1960s, possibly because the traditional 'two weeks by the seaside' which had been part of the British way of life for so long,

Codeg dolls

was beginning to go out of fashion. Instead, many people were risking life and limb to holiday in France, Germany or Spain. And, to prove they had been there, they brought home a costume doll.

In addition, England itself was becoming very touristy, especially London, and so shops in the areas frequented by visitors tended to be filled with plastic dolls dressed as policemen, beefeaters or guardsmen – the fact that England had no national costume wasn't a deterrent for manufacturers. Whilst Rogark and other makers continued producing their Welsh ladies and Scottish boys, they were joined by manufacturers such as Rexard and Almar, and importers Cowan de Groot, using the trade name Codeg, who made not just English costume dolls, but dolls wearing costumes from all around the globe. Many of these could be bought in Woolworths for 2/6d (12½p) or so, meaning that even if you never went abroad, you could still boast an interesting collection of dolls from other lands! I clearly remember going into Woolworths, aged around fifteen, and buying an Eskimo in a blue suit with a white fluffy-trimmed hood, an Indian lady in a light blue sari and a Native American with a feather headdress. These sleep-eyed dolls, about 8 inches high, were made from hard plastic but were unmarked. They are still in excellent condition after all this time, a tribute to the materials used (see Chapter 9).

Vinyl

Not long after the Second World War ended, by the late 1940s, the majority of doll manufacturers in Britain had switched to the use of plastic, as explained in my book *British Dolls of the 1950s*. However, the last few years of the 1950s saw further developments in the field of plastics, and a new, softer plastic material was introduced, which we usually refer to as vinyl. Vinyl was regarded as the perfect medium for dolls, because it was virtually unbreakable. It could be moulded to show dimples, creases and wrinkles, and was lightweight and warm to the touch. Being flexible, vinyl could take inner armatures enabling dolls to hold a pose, and could be dunked in the bath without harm. Best of all, though, nylon hair could be inserted, using special machines, directly into a doll's head, which meant that the hair could be brushed and combed without fear of strands falling out or a wig coming unstuck. Now, dolls didn't need to have moulded hair under their wigs (a common sight in the 1950s, as it meant a doll could still have hair, even when the wig was lost), and they really could be shampooed, showered or immersed in the bath.

Also, as dolls were at last virtually unbreakable (the hard plastic types could still crack or break if they fell), they could now 'do things' – they could be more active, as in the case of 'Tippy Tumbles', who could turn somersaults without risk of harm to her head. Manufacturers gradually became more creative, realising that vinyl allowed them much more freedom of design. With hindsight, we now realise that this was the true beginning of the 'throwaway' doll trend; they were gradually becoming more affordable – although, compared to nowadays, 1960s' dolls were still not cheap. As they became more robust, by some paradox they also became expendable and less respected. Girls might have a dozen or so dolls of various types and sizes, whereas before they would only have a few, which they treasured.

Large Teens

The early 1960s saw a spate of large-sized fashion dolls; as yet, the idea of the small teen Barbie-size doll hadn't particularly caught on in Britain, and so the teen dolls tended to be more like shapely large play dolls. Standing around 15 inches to 20 inches high, some had been introduced in the late 1950s, but the heyday for these dolls seems to have been around 1961/2. They were produced by most of the major companies, such as Pedigree, Palitoy, Chiltern, Roddy, Rosebud and Faerie Glen.

Chiltern teen doll

These dolls are intriguing, because they demonstrate so clearly how the teens of the very early sixties were dressing just like their mothers. They wear flared skirts, plant-pot shaped hats, duster coats, fitted jackets, shirt-waisted dresses, tailored blouses and pretty cotton summer frocks. Their shapely legs are encased in nylon stockings, and they invariably have strappy high-heeled sandals. Often the outfits are complemented with pearl earrings or necklaces. No jeans or sneakers here; everything is so formal – little did we realise that within a couple of years a dramatic change would take place as the sixties took hold. When that happened, it was as though a magic wand had been waved, causing teens to suddenly appear in jeans, bright colours and 'dolly bird' dresses – it was as if, overnight, the teenager had evolved!

So these large teen dolls are a vital link in the fashion chain; they depict not only the clothes which the late fifties/early sixties young girl wore, but also mark the end of the formality and the dress code. No longer would teens dress as their parents did, from now on they would have their own styles. The significance of these larger fashion dolls shouldn't be underrated – though nowadays not so popular with collectors as are the smaller teen dolls such as Sindy and Tressy from the same decade, they clearly show the dramatic way in which young fashion changed direction.

Chiltern

This name was used by H.G. Stone and Company, a subsidiary of L. Rees and Company. Leon Rees had been active in the doll world since the 1900s, also producing plush toys and teddy bears. Both dolls and animals were of excellent quality (see Chapter 4).

AN IN-DEPTH LOOK AT A CHILTERN TEEN

Unlike many of the other large teens of the era, Chiltern marked most of their dolls, so they are easy to recognise and identify. The teens were actually first made in the late 1950s, but were very popular in the 1960s until the smaller, Sindy-sized dolls were introduced by various companies, and the larger teens fell into disfavour.

Chiltern teens came in several sizes – this is a 15½ inch model, which seems to have been the most popular size, as they are still quite easy to find today. Her pleasant face features blue sleep-eyes with long lashes, and she has high arched eyebrows. Her small, well-shaped mouth is closed and her ears are not pierced. Her slim body features a hint of a bust (unlike Barbie, British teens were usually far less curvaceous) and she has elegant curved hands with painted nails. Her feet are arched to take high-heeled sandals, and her toenails are painted, too.

This particular doll has short blonde rooted hair styled in a bubble cut, and wears a pretty, but unpretentious, cotton day dress in a typical

Chiltern teen doll

early 60s' style. The dress, bearing a pattern of red stars and blue flowers, has a full skirt, fitted bodice and a large collar trimmed with a turquoise band. Interestingly, the collar is separate and is attached to the dress by two poppers. She is marked 'Chiltern Made in England' on the back of her neck.

Other Chiltern teen sizes available were a larger, 19-inch doll and a smaller, 11-inch example which was known as 'Ballerina', though it did not wear a tutu. Various outfits were available for the Chiltern teens, and they were nicely-made dolls which used quality vinyl, as were all those from this particular company.

Faerie Glen

Hook and Franks Ltd. used the trademark Faerie Glen on their dolls as well as on their extensive range of dolls' clothes. Founded just after the Second World War by Daisy Franks and her daughter Peggy – a world champion table-tennis player who later became a presenter of the popular television show *Blue Peter* – it was the outfits for which the company was truly famed. They were of excellent quality and style, and were made for many sizes and types of doll. Each tiny garment had a silk label bearing the Faerie Glen name and a picture of a fairy.

The outfits were sold in their thousands, and were still available in shops in the 1980s, their labels making them easy to identify. Many of the earlier dresses had unusual white plastic flat loop fastenings. Because the clothes span several decades, it is interesting to see how the fashions changed, from the formality of nylon stockings and tailored dresses in the early 1960s to the colourful casuals of the 70s and 80s (see Chapter 7).

The Faerie Glen teen dolls came in several sizes, amongst them being Gigi, who at 15 inches, seems to have been the most popular, but others included 20-inch Jackie, and Tina, who was a Sindy-size teen. Gigi and Jackie were unmarked, and their most outstanding features were their large shimmering eyes. Unlike many other companies' teen dolls, Gigi and Jackie had unpainted finger and toenails.

Gigi by Faerie Glen

Palitoy

Palitoy was a trading name of Cascelloid, which was formed in 1919 by Alfred Pallett. Originally the company made household items from celluloid, producing their first dolls, celluloid representations of various Mabel Lucy Attwell characters, in 1925. In 1937, Cascelloid became a subsidiary of British Xylonite Ltd., and acquired a factory at Coalville, Leicester. Later, this was to become famed as the home of thousands of attractive, well-designed dolls. Cascelloid experimented with composition, producing a range of virtually unbreakable 'Plastex' dolls, and began using the 'Palitoy' trademark, derived from Alfred Pallet's surname, in the 1930s.

By the 1960s the company were producing a wide range of attractive, well-made dolls, and were quick to embrace new procedures and discoveries. Their 'Tiny Tears' doll (see Chapter 5) was a classic which topped the best-selling girls' toy charts for many years. In 1968, Palitoy was acquired by the US company General Mills, though continued to use their own name.

The Palitoy teen range embraced many dolls, with pretty names such as Annette, Debbie, Arline, Renee, Deirdre and Janine. The dolls had a dainty look, with slender limbs and elegant fingers, and the nails were unpainted. Writer Colette Mansell, who has extensively studied these dolls, discovered that some of them are marked with a tiny, often faint circle, containing the words 'Made in England' in minute letters, just above the waist. In her book on teen fashion dolls, (see Further Reading) Colette also describes a beautiful and rare 20-inch high black teen doll, Luana, dressed in a Hawaiian outfit. One of the most unusual of the Palitoy teens was Nurse Carol (see Chapter 6).

Pedigree

The Pedigree trade name was used by the Tri-ang company, founded by three brothers just after the First World War. The brothers were named Lines, and they built up a huge empire of factories. By the 1960s, the dolls produced by the company were probably the most elite of the time, and of excellent quality and design (see Chapter 6). Their most famed

Pedigree teen doll

contribution during this period, however, was the introduction of the Sindy doll in 1963 (see Chapter 3). Tri-ang also sold a range of Mam'selle doll's outfits (see Chapter 7).

Just like many other companies at the time, Pedigree introduced a range of large teenage dolls, which continued to be made until the mid-sixties. They were available as both 15-inch and 20-inch high girls, all given names such as Merle, Rosalie, Myrtle and Marilyn, though sadly unmarked. Although they wore the Pedigree signature logo brooch, these were normally soon lost. A further series, Debutante, was more expensive. These dolls wore really elegant and well-detailed fashions from the period, such as a glamorous, full-skirted spotted dress with a toning stole, bag and hat, or an elegant pink satin ball-gown finished with a large bow at the back hem, complete with a white fur stole. There was also Little Miss Vogue, a distinctive 10-inch high doll, who held her arms rather awkwardly out at her sides. However, in 1963, the company's latest teen, Sindy, burst onto the scene – and was so successful, that very soon no-one wanted the larger teen dolls. After that, most manufacturers switched to making smaller teens.

Roddy

This trademark was used by D.G. Todd and Company, founded after the Second World War, and based in Southport, Lancashire, though Daniel Todd had been managing director of a Southport toy company since the 1930s. Famed in the 1950s for its comprehensive range of Roddy dolls, it continued well into the 1960s before changing its name in 1969 (see Chapter 6).

The Roddy dolls were sold in 14/15-inch and 19-inch sizes, and were usually marked on the back of the neck. They came with a variety of rooted hair styles, and some featured jointed waists and painted nails. Roddy teens wore a selection of in-vogue styles, with plenty of full skirts, duster coats and posh evening gowns; the early 1960s' dolls had names such as Kym and Cindy, and, as with most of the various manufacturers' ranges, included a beautiful Bride doll dressed in white satin with a net veil.

Rosebud

Founded in the late 1940s, initially this company was known as Nene Plastics, but the Rosebud trade name was registered in 1947 by T. Eric Smith, the owner. The company was situated at Raunds, Northampton-shire, but in 1960 a new factory was built at Wellingborough (see Chapter 6).

A flip through a Rosebud catalogue of the 1960s reveals some very interesting teen dolls, including a range with coloured hair. Their tallest teens were 20 inches high, and included a blonde girl described as a 'Very smart teenager with modern hair style and many accessories including nylon stockings, high-heeled shoes and drop earrings. Available in 2 colours'. She cost 70/9 (£3.53), and wore a blue dress with a duster coat. The coat featured a large flowery design, matching the 'upturned flowerpot-style' hat, and she wore white heeled sandals. Her hair was short and rather bouffant, and her formal attire is a million miles away from that worn by the casually-dressed teen of today.

A bride is also featured. 'This radiant bride wears a ballerina length dress of white nylon lace. She has pearl earrings and carries a colourful bouquet

Rosebud teen doll

of flowers. She also has several pretty petticoats (including one of paper nylon), stockings and high-heeled shoes.' This brunette, again with short hair – all of the dolls illustrated in the catalogue had similar hair – sold for 76/- (£3.80).

Amongst the slightly shorter, 15-inch, teen dolls in the catalogue is a girl in a gingham dress available with either blue or pink hair, a blonde in a sweater and 'wool tartan trews' and another with a choice of three hair colours, dressed in a red blouse and a full skirt printed with large red roses. Many of these dolls were also available in the 20-inch size. The smallest teens in the Rosebud catalogue were just 8½ inches tall, made from soft vinyl with superfine rooted hair and sleeping eyes. Available in a choice of three hair colours, they came wearing a bra and pants, all ready to be dressed either at home, or in one of the many dresses made by Rosebud or other doll companies.

An In-Depth Look At A Rosebud Teen

This doll, at 15 inches tall, is one of the smaller models. Her shapely body and legs are of hard plastic, while her head and arms are of a very soft, almost rubbery, form of vinyl. Her rooted hair – which was originally pale blue but has faded over the years – is rooted and arranged in a short bouffant style, and she has thin curved brows, 'real' lashes and a small closed mouth. Her fingernails are painted red and her feet are arched so that she can wear high heels. She is unmarked, but there is no doubt she is by Rosebud as she is shown in the 1961 catalogue.

Her light blue cotton gingham shirt-waisted dress has a full skirt and fastens at the back with two white poppers. A white plastic belt fits snugly around her waist. Underneath she wears a cream lace-trimmed silky taffeta petticoat and matching knickers. There is no bra, and no mention of one in the catalogue. Her stockings – not tights, in the early 1960s they didn't come in till the miniskirt made them imperative – have seams up the back of the legs. Her dainty white plastic sandals have tiny flower motifs.

Other Rosebud teens include a fabulous 15-inch pink-haired doll dressed ready for a formal dance in a beautiful pink ultra-full-skirted gown patterned with golden glitter, complete with a matching sequin-

Rosebud teen doll

Rosebud pink-haired teen doll

trimmed stole. Her skirt bears a silver 'Rosebud' logo in script. Around her neck is a sparkling diamante flower necklace on a chain, and she has diamante earrings. On her head is an elaborate tiara made from twisted golden wire.

Winfield

Many major retailers used their own brand names, often selling dolls under them, such as Tesco's 'Delaware' or British Home Stores' 'Prova'. In the 1960s, Woolworths took the name Winfield – Frank Woolworth's middle name – and adopted it as a brand name to use on all of their own ranges.

Amongst items to use the name were 'Little Beauty' dressed dolls, which appeared as both girls and beautiful teen dolls and were introduced in 1964 (see Chapter 7). Of exceptional quality, Little Beauty dolls were deservedly popular, and featured rooted, soft, shiny hair. They were made from a soft touch vinyl with an attractive finish, and were, of course, completely washable.

AN IN-DEPTH LOOK AT A WINFIELD LITTLE BEAUTY TEEN

Standing 15 inches tall, this dainty teen really lives up to her 'Little Beauty' name. She has blue sleep-eyes with 'real' thick hair upper lashes and painted lower lashes. Her closed coral pink mouth is quite solemn, her

Winfield 'Little Beauty' teen doll

cheeks feature a delightful blush and she has pierced ears from which hang tiny pearl earrings. Little Beauty has blonde, short, rooted Saran hair, a teen-shaped body with a small bust, twist waist and her fingernails have a hint of a tint. The doll is totally unmarked.

She wears a lilac print cotton, full-skirted dress, trimmed at the neck with lace, and with elasticated elbow-length sleeves. Underneath, she wears white cotton lace-edged panties and seamed stockings. Her high-heeled sandals are white. Attached to her wrist is a swing tag which reads, 'Little Beauty vinyl doll'.

The other side of the tag reads, 'Little Beauty has saran rooted hair which can be shampooed, brushed, combed and styled. Note: Because of the doll's texture it can be easily wiped or washed. Made in England. Regd. Design.'

So many of these larger teens are unmarked, which can make them extremely difficult to attribute to one particular maker. It's always a bonus to find one in the original box, or bearing original hang tags or other provenance.

Large teen modelling 1960s' rain outfit, including overshoes

Chapter 3

Small Teens

As a general rule, British teens tended to be more unsophisticated than their US counterparts; the American tradition of formality with glamorous 'prom dresses' worn at school dances was alien, unless they came from the upper social classes where the debutante social round still ruled. This didn't mean that British youngsters never dressed up – of course they did – but, unless attending a wedding, christening or similar affair, the lace frocks, posh hats and silky gloves were on their way out. As we saw in Chapter 2, the first couple of years of the decade still kept some formality, but jeans and cotton tops were the chosen casual garb for most of the decade – although smart suits or neat dresses were still the general rule for the workplace.

Barbie had been created in 1959 in America by Ruth Handler, based on a German doll Lilli (see Chapter 10). Lilli was based on a Bild Lilli cartoon, centred, unfortunately, around an outspoken, sexy young woman, a 'sex pet for mature males', and consequently not quite the doll you would give your young daughter. Though Barbie was occasionally seen in Britain, her hard looks, heavy make-up, glamorous clothes and overall sophistication didn't really appeal to children in the UK. In addition, her vital statistics were extremely vital – translating at 42, 22, 36, they were rather over the top. So when the Pedigree company introduced a wholesome, fresh-faced teen doll, wearing an outfit of blue denim jeans, a striped top and sneakers, she was a tremendous hit. In keeping with the youthful look, her figure was a more modest 32, 24, 35. Sindy, launched in September 1963, reflected modern British youth, and was very soon a star.

Tammy

However, Sindy had a doppelganger in America. Tammy was a teen doll issued by the Ideal Toy Company in 1962, and she too featured short honey-blonde hair, side-glance eyes and a shy smile. Furthermore, her slogan was 'The doll you love to dress', which was Sindy's slogan here. So, according to the Americans, Sindy was nothing more than a Tammy clone. At the time, Pedigree claimed otherwise! Tammy had a sister, Pepper, and a boyfriend, Bud.

It wasn't long before Sindy had a sister and a boyfriend too. Even so, Sindy had something very special going for her, something which Tammy lacked. Sindy was the first smaller-size British heavily promoted teen doll, and consequently, her launch created quite a stir. She was the British equivalent of Barbie, and was soon a top seller, with hundreds of fashions, accessories and tie-ins. By contrast, Tammy was phased out in 1966. Today, Sindy, though now completely different in style and having undergone several changes of manufacturer, is still sold in Britain, although because of the numerous other teens on the market, she has lost her

Tammy by Ideal

tremendous impact. Now she is just another doll, and usually passed over in favour of a heavily-made-up, bling-laden Bratz.

Sindy

Girls in the 1960s didn't grow up quite as quickly as they do nowadays, and so it wasn't regarded as strange for girls in their early teens to buy a Sindy doll. Unlike today, where fashion dolls are targeted for sale to three-year-olds, Sindy was marketed as a doll to appeal to older girls. Pedigree had come up with a brilliant, yet simple concept – for decades boys had collected toy soldiers, small cars and farm animals, but the collecting arena for girls had been neglected. Suddenly, this innovative idea had arrived; a doll with masses of accessories, friends, clothes and other tie-ins. When manufacturers realised the scope of this previously untapped wealth, they soon turned it to their advantage. Now, girls could spend their pocket money on numerous outfits and items for Sindy, as well as for the other teens which appeared in Sindy's wake.

First Sindy, Pedigree

AN IN-DEPTH LOOK AT A SINDY DOLL

The very first, 1963, Sindy stood 12 inches tall and was jointed at neck, shoulders and hips. Her head, which was quite large, felt rubbery, and her body and legs were made from a thin, hollow hard plastic. Her arms were of a rubber-type plastic. She featured painted side-glance eyes with three lashes at the outer corners, a small pert nose and red lips. The back of her head was marked 'Made in England'. Her short, bobbed hair – which came in three colours, blonde, brunette or auburn – was kept tidy by an Alice band, just like those which thousands of British children wore at the time. Sindy was dressed in an outfit known as 'Weekenders'. It comprised a patriotic-looking red, white and blue striped long-sleeved top, blue denim jeans and white sneakers. The top was fastened with flat white poppers marked 'Made in England'.

Two years later, Sindy was slightly updated and given bendy arms and legs, and she seemed to have more facial colouring, especially in her cheeks. In 1966, another update improved the vinyl quality and also gave

New Look Sindy, Pedigree   **Walking Sindy, Pedigree**

her a highly-coloured face, making for an exceptionally pretty doll. This Sindy was marked 'Made in Hong Kong' on her back, and as well as the previous three hair colours, she could also be obtained with black hair. The hair was still short, and she still wore the Weekenders outfit.

1968 saw the 'New Look Sindy', whose hair was now shoulder-length and featured a side parting. She had 'real' eyelashes and a twisty waist, which made her much more poseable. This Sindy was sold in different outfits, including 'Ice Skater' and 'Fashion Girl', and she was marked 'Made in Hong Kong' on the back of her head. Very similar was the 'Walking Sindy', issued in 1969. This doll had longer, bendy rubber legs which had discs on the hip joints; the idea was to make the legs swing freely to create a walking action. She came in three hair colours. Walking Sindy was sold in a navy and red spot jacket

'Miniature' Sindy, Pedigree

with matching skirt and a red sleeveless jumper, and the first Walking Sindys, known to today's collectors as 'Sideparts' due to their hairstyles, were also given a free yellow coat featuring a flowery belt, collar and cuffs.

Another 1960s' doll, referred to as a 'Pin Head' or 'Miniature' Sindy by collectors, was 1½ inches shorter than the other dolls and made from hard vinyl. She was marked 'Made in Hong Kong'. I understand that these 'Miniatures' were due to the way Sindy was made. She was cast from copper head-moulds which were mounted onto a 'spider', liquid vinyl was squirted in, and then the whole thing revolved in an oven until the vinyl was cooked and set.

New moulds would be taken from the original moulds, and these would be slightly smaller, eventually resulting in the Miniature dolls. The differences in appearance (sometimes Sindy looks unnaturally pale) and in the types of plastic were due to plastic quality – it was necessary for Pedigree to economise as much as possible, and so the plastic wasn't always consistent. Also, sometimes the bodies were blow-moulded, which could result in very thin plastic. Many of the Hong Kong-produced dolls were made from a harder plastic mix.

Tuffin and Foale

Sindy's 'Weekenders' outfit was designed by Tuffin and Foale, as were several of her other garments. Sally Tuffin and Marion Foale were famed designers, leading lights in the modern fashion industry, with a shop in trendy Carnaby Street. They are credited with being the designers who popularised the trouser suit, an innovative idea at the time which created

Tuffin and Foale

an enormous stir, especially when women began to wear the creations to the office.

Sally Tuffin explained that she and Marion Foale were chosen to design the Sindy outfits because 'Foale & Tuffin were the fashion designers of the day and very much flavour of the month, being of the same age as those they were designing clothes for. It must have seemed a natural course of action for Pedigree Dolls to want these names for their outfits. The jeans, T-shirt and sneakers look of Weekenders was definitely the fashion of the time and the manufacturers were keen that Sindy was seen to be "up-to-date" with the latest trends. The patriotic appearance of Weekenders came into being because the Union Jack was the big thing during this time and the design evolved accordingly.'

However, Marion isn't quite so sure that they had a completely free hand with Weekenders. 'It was a long time ago,' she said, 'and to be honest, it could be that we didn't have quite as much input into that outfit. I don't really remember. When we were asked to design clothes for Sindy, it wasn't a big deal. It was almost a flippant thing – we didn't put great importance upon it. I do remember "Shopping in the Rain", "Lunch Date" and the skiing outfit (Winter Holiday). We had problems with that one. We couldn't just design what we wanted – Pedigree asked us to make outfits for various themes which they suggested, such as wet weather or skiing holidays. It was an unusual thing to be asked – to design clothes for a doll. I don't know, now, what our reactions were, but I do remember thinking

'Shopping in the Rain'

how vulgar Barbie was, and not wanting Sindy to be like that.'

Marion went on to explain how they set about designing clothes for a small doll: 'In a way, it was like designing for a person, a three-dimensional form. We modelled the fabric onto the doll, snipping around until it was right. Then we would make a toile pattern, and then a paper pattern, before producing the sample costume.' Marion couldn't really remember all the outfits which she and Sally had created, while Sally said that she didn't have a preference, adding, 'Each design was "of the moment" so it is very difficult to nominate a favourite. It is very flattering to know that collectors are still interested in our Sindy designs, especially as Sindy was launched in the UK with our Weekenders design.'

'If only we had hindsight,' remarked Marion, 'we might have continued with Sindy. We never thought that the doll would continue for so long, that she would be so big. I am totally gobsmacked that, forty-five years later, collectors still want to know about our Sindy designs.' Today, the

Pedigree Sindy

names of Tuffin and Foale are still very much esteemed in the creative world – Sally Tuffin is a designer of exquisite pottery at Dennis China Works, while Marion Foale designs and produces exclusive knitwear.

According to an ex-Pedigree employee, because the company sold Sindy for the first four years dressed just in 'Weekenders', with other outfits available separately, Pedigree probably lost out on thousands of sales – later they realised that girls wanted more than one doll, but didn't want them all wearing the same clothes. Then they began selling Sindy dressed in a choice of apparel.

Sindy on the Scene

Sindy's innocent, natural looks meant that she gave full rein to a child's imagination and could be whatever age a child wanted – friend, sister, mother or the girl next door. Her casual clothes were the kind of clothes they would wear, too.

When the Sindy doll had been announced to the retail trade, the majority of toy stockists turned down the idea. As there were so many large teen dolls on the market, they couldn't understand why anyone would want to buy a small, 12-inch fashion doll. They decided there would be no call for her, but were soon proved wrong when an intensive television advertising campaign turned Sindy into a household name – the shops were bombarded with requests for the doll. The Pedigree company must have been delighted. Sindy was

'Dream Date'

literally an overnight success, and her slogan, 'The Doll You Love To Dress', though pinched from Tammy, quickly became inseparable from Sindy in the minds of the British public.

Sindy was aimed at the 5–12 age group, and she wasn't a particularly cheap doll – in fact, many children were disappointed on being told by their parents that they couldn't have one, or worse still, would have to

Sindy by Pedigree, mint in box

have a 'clone'. (Sindy lookalikes soon flooded shops and market stalls, often even wearing copies of the Weekenders outfit.) It was a blow after seeing all the television adverts. At the time, Sindy cost 22/6 (£1.13p), and the costumes – a vital part of the fun of the doll – were also relatively expensive. Actually, it wasn't just Sindy which was pricey; in the 1960s most toy prices were high, mainly due to retail price maintenance. The result was that, unlike today when toys are often ridiculously cheap, thus enabling a child to regularly buy new ones, a sixties' child would probably own only a couple of fashion dolls, hence there are so many early Sindys still around which have been carefully and lovingly played with.

Although the 'Swinging Sixties' had arrived, not all of Britain was

**Sindy and
Patch clones**

affected; much of the country was still traditionalist. This might seem an odd notion today, but at the time ideas and trends were not instantaneous, and the north/south divide really was a gulf. When The Beatles first burst onto the scene, southerners were amazed by their Liverpool accents and the way they pronounced words such as 'bus' and 'bath'. Likewise, Janice Nichols, a panellist on the 1960s' pop music show, *Thank Your Lucky Stars* became notorious purely because of her pronunciation. Birmingham-born Janice remarked of a record, 'Oi'll give it foive,' causing those 'down south' to throw up their hands in amazement, being used to the refined, neutral accents used extensively in the media.

Accordingly, for the first few years of Sindy's life, her clothes were rather traditional, and slightly behind the times in terms of the London teen styles. Girls in London might have taken to miniskirts and op art dresses, but initially, many of the Sindy-owning girls still aspired to dress like their mothers. Sindy took a few years before all her outfits were at the very cutting-edge of fashion.

Sindy Outfits

As befitting 'The Doll You Love To Dress', there were soon plenty of outfits and accessories to collect, though as already mentioned, these were not cheap to buy. For example, 'Skating Girl' (a circular red skirt, red tights, striped white,

'Lunch Date'

black and red sweater, and matching hat and scarf, complete with skating boots and mittens), cost 15/3 (77p), while 'Winter Holiday' (fur-trimmed blue quilted anorak, red trews, white polo neck jumper, lace-up boots, skis, ski poles, mittens and sunglasses) was 23/3 (£1.17), almost the cost of the basic 'Weekenders' doll. Additional outfits included 'Beauty Queen', (long white flocked skirt, red fur-trimmed bodice, printed sash and coronet), Bridesmaid's Dress (long lemon short-sleeved dress, flowery headband, posy, pearl necklace and white shoes), as well as nurse, air hostess and pony club outfits.

Amongst the other early outfits were 'Lunch Date' (a Tuffin and Foale creation made to look like a black turtleneck sweater and green tartan skirt, accessorised with a tartan headscarf, handbag and black shoes) and 'Shopping in the Rain' (also by Tuffin and Foale). This was a very fashionable shiny black PVC coat with matching headscarf, red handbag, red wellies and an umbrella. 'Country Walk' had Sindy back in tartan again, this time a brown check. She teamed it with a brown suede jacket, green jumper and brown brogues, and had a strange little dog made from pipe cleaners, called Ringo after The Beatles' drummer.

Paul

In 1965, Pedigree decided that Sindy needed a boyfriend. They called him Paul, probably because the name 'Paul' belonged to the most popular Beatle. It must be said that the first Paul doll did have a rather wimpish look, though in a sweet way! I can remember the first time I saw the doll. I was on holiday as a teen, in Devon, in 1966, and was amazed to think that a Sindy doll had been given a boyfriend. It was something that I had never come across before, never having even seen Barbie, who by then would have been quite settled with her Ken. The teen dolls which had been familiar to me in the late fifties were all doomed to remain spinsters!

Paul was 12½ inches high, and featured moulded hair, painted brown. He had painted brown eyes, bendable arms and legs and was unmarked. He was sold wearing a red jumper, pair of blue denim jeans and white shoes. A year later, a doll which collectors refer to as 'Miniature Paul' arrived. He was around half an inch shorter than the previous doll, and

was marked 'Made in Hong Kong'. His legs were made of a hard plastic, and his head was much smaller than the 1966 Paul doll. He seemed to be made from a much pinker plastic than the first Paul. In 1967, Paul was given 'real' rooted hair. He was marked 'Made in Hong Kong', and had bendy limbs. He looked fairly similar to the first Paul, apart from the hair. Sadly for Sindy, Paul departed from the scene shortly after, and didn't re-appear till the 1980s.

Paul had a selection of outfits, too, such as 'Motorway Man' (an all-the-rage suede motoring jacket with fur collar, teamed with brown check trousers and Chelsea boots), 'London Look' (a very smart navy wool suit with a light blue shirt, slim tie) and 'And So To Bed' (a rather strange blue stripey outfit consisting of pyjamas and a collarless dressing-gown. The accessories were fun, though – a spongebag containing a super 'electric' razor, toothbrush, toothpaste, comb, brush, soap and face cloth). He also had a white T-shirt with a big red 'P' on the front, a snazzy pair of swimming trunks, and yachting, tennis and football outfits.

Patch

Sindy was given a young sister, 'That Rascal, Patch!' in 1966, and though she was only around for six years she made a huge impact on the Sindy world. Today, many collectors concentrate solely on Patch, and both the doll and her clothes are eagerly sought after. This delightful little girl stood 8½"–9½" tall (her height varied depending on the factory), and featured side-glance

Paul with rooted hair by Pedigree

eyes looking to the left, a slight smile and freckles – quantity and shape depended on where the doll was made. At first, Patch was produced at Pedigree's Merton factory, and then for a while was made in Hong Kong before returning to Britain, this time to Pedigree's Canterbury works.

Patch by Pedigree, in dungarees

One of the nicest things about Patch, and which maybe accounts for much of her popularity, is that each doll appears slightly different – hair colours, hairstyles, facial colouring, and amount of freckles all vary, giving each doll an individuality. Her hair came in several shades, and the most common were blonde, brown and auburn. Initially, the hair on the British dolls was made from Saran and styled in a short, straight bob, though the later Canterbury dolls had a more curly style and the hair was finer. Earlier

**Patch by Pedigree in 'Water
Wings' outfit**

**Patch, by Pedigree, in Brownie
outfit**

dolls were marked 'Made in England', while the later types bore the number 047001.

At first, the Patch dolls made in Hong Kong had coarse hair, but this was soon changed to a characteristic very silky fibre. These dolls were marked 'Made in Hong Kong', and they often featured brighter face paint than the British dolls. It does seem, though, that often the British dolls have more character to their faces, which could be due to the hand-painting, especially of the freckles. Naturally, as with Sindy, Patch clones were available in the shops for those whose pocket money couldn't stretch to the real thing.

Most collectors are familiar with the distinctive Patch outfit – she was originally sold wearing an all-in-one outfit made to resemble a pair of blue denim dungarees over a red-checked, short-sleeved top. On her left knee was sewn a gingham patch – very occasionally, this patch has been found on the right knee of the dungarees, consequently causing quite a stir in the collectors' market, with the garment selling for much more than usual. She also wore white slip-on shoes and a red-checked headscarf.

Patch was around until 1972 before finally being discontinued, but today she is a tremendous favourite with Sindy collectors. Yet according to a Pedigree spokesman, Patch, as well as Paul and the other friends, were poor sellers when compared to Sindy. With hindsight, apparently, Patch would probably never have been produced; not only a great loss to the doll world, but to Sindy too, who must have enjoyed having her little sister around!

Other outfits issued to Patch – over thirty in all – included a party dress, Brownie uniform, school uniform, ballet tutu, swimming costume, raincoat and various separates. Some outfits seem to be more frequently found than others, for instance, 'Home For the Day' (a black and white checked pinafore), 'Birthday Party' (red cloak worn over a black velvet dress trimmed with beige lace), 'Brownie' (complete Brownie uniform bearing a badge of the 'First Merton Pack'), 'Schooldays' (brown gymslip with shirt, coat, hat and satchel), and 'Water Wings' (navy swimsuit and accessories). Patch's outfits sold for various prices – in 1967, the cheapest was a yellow raincoat, sou'wester and black

Swan Lake Patch

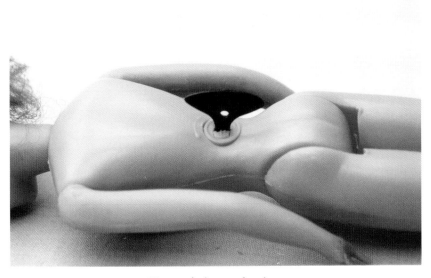

Tressy hair mechanism

wellies at 13/9 (68p), while the dearest, 'Schooldays' was 25/3 (£1.27) – more than the Patch doll, who was selling at 21/11 (£1.10).

Lucky Patch had a pony, called Pixie, which was, as the box proudly proclaimed, 'complete with saddle, bridle, stirrups and brushable mane' and she also acquired two friends, Betsy and Poppet in 1968, which are much harder to find than – as she was known – 'That Rascal, Patch!'

Tressy

Probably Sindy's main rival in the 1960s was Tressy, a 12-inch teen introduced by the Palitoy company in 1964, and who soon proved popular. The doll was produced under licence from the American Character Doll Company, and owed her success to one very special feature – her hair could grow! Tressy, rather like Barbie, was another big girl, with statistics equivalent to 38, 21, 35 – the waist size, in particular, was suspect!

A major advertising promotion had everyone repeating the slogan, 'But HOW does Tressy's hair grow?', and, apparently, little girls who owned a

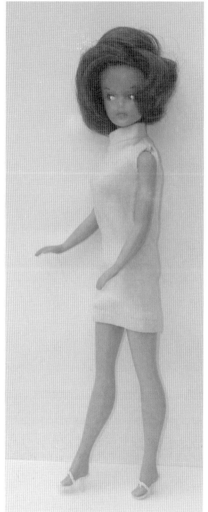
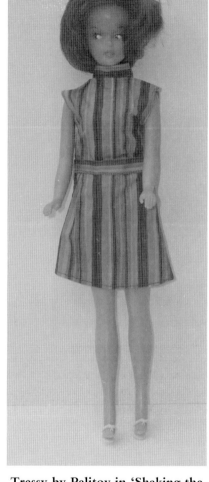

Tressy by Palitoy

Tressy by Palitoy in 'Shaking the Night Away' outfit

Tressy, and consequently were 'in the know', took great delight in passing on the secret to a few chosen friends; if you didn't know how Tressy's hair grew, you became something of a social outcast. Every young girl wanted a Tressy doll; it seemed miraculous that a doll could really grow her own hair.

Tressy's hair grew when a button was pushed in her tummy. The button released a 'magic strand', which could be gently pulled until the doll's hair lengthened. When Tressy's hair needed to be shortened, the strand was rewound into the head by means of a small metal key which could be inserted into a hole in her back. As the key tended to become mislaid, later versions of the doll had a plastic key as a permanent fixture.

There were several versions of Tressy issued over the eighteen years or so that she was produced. The first UK doll had painted, side-glance eyes looking towards the right, and she was jointed at neck, shoulders and hips. Her legs were straight and didn't bend at all. She had mid-length rooted hair in various colours, without a fringe, and was made of a poor quality vinyl – rather surprising as Palitoy products were usually excellent. Often, the Tressy heads tended to fade, and some dolls found today are extremely pale. She was dressed in a blue, lemon or pink straight shift dress with a belt, and she wore white shoes. Sometimes she had an American Character mark on her neck, but more usually was unmarked.

Just as with Sindy, plenty of additional outfits were available for Tressy, including party dresses, shift dresses, underclothes, a nightdress, skiing outfit, swimming costume, coat, trousers and tops. Although Tressy was a great rival of Sindy, she never managed to outsell her, and never had the extensive range of clothes and accessories which Sindy boasted. In the late 1960s she was updated and given front-facing eyes and a fringe.

Tressy updated version late 1960s, by Palitoy

Toots by Palitoy

A 1967 catalogue advertises Tressy for sale at 30/6 (£1.53): 'Introducing Tressy – the model. Slim and attractive with vinyl head and arms. Complete with a smart yellow jersey shift dress, chain belt, panties, shoes, hairgrips and special display stand and key. Hair styling leaflet provided. 12 inches tall.' Several outfits appear in the same catalogue, and include 'Winter Journey' (red shift dress and black and white check coat with fur trim), 'In the Office' (red corduroy pinafore dress over a green and black shirt) and 'Air Hostess' (blue cotton uniform with matching cap). The outfits sold for various prices, ranging from 14/3 (71p) to 17/9 (88p).

Jeanette Nott from Plymouth remembers, 'When I was about twelve my cousin Joy lived with us. She was two years younger than me; we slept in the same room. I remember waking up that Christmas to my lovely Tressy, and recall the smell of brand new plastic. Joy had her blonde Sindy. I don't remember much else about the day. It was lovely when I discovered the Internet as I found my Tressy and Joy's Sindy: it has its uses; it can bring memories of things you had forgotten, it certainly has for me. I saw an advert for Sindy wallpaper on there and I thought, Oh my! I remember having that wallpaper on my bedroom wall. I have since acquired a roll through the Internet!'

Tressy was given a younger sister, Toots, in 1965 and a friend, Mary Make-Up, in 1967. Toots featured the same grow-hair ability as her sister,

**Mary Make-Up
by Palitoy**

but was smaller at 9 inches. She too had painted side-glance eyes, looking
to the right. She came in a white ballet tutu with white ballet slippers, and
there were many outfits available to buy separately. One of the cutest was
'Poodle Parade', a checked frock which came with two plastic poodles –
a breed of dog which was still very much the rage in the sixties, just as it
was in the fifties. Toots sold at 25/6 (£1.27) and most of her outfits were
10/3 (51p).

Mary Make-Up was a very plain-looking doll, deliberately so, as the whole idea was to emphasise her features with the make-up supplied with her. The make-up could be used to tint her hair, paint her eyes, lips or cheeks, and to colour her nails – then it all could be washed off again. Mary's eyes were front-facing, and her hair was styled in a short fashionable bouffant bob. Although of a similar vinyl to Tressy, her face had a special finish to ensure the make-up wouldn't sink into the plastic. She wore an eye-catching royal blue or scarlet shift dress featuring white stripe detail on the sleeves and a matching hairband and, at 12 inches tall, was the same height as Tressy. No other outfits were issued specifically for Mary Make-Up; she was expected to share Tressy clothes, and the packets were labelled with both dolls' names.

Sindy and 'That Rascal, Patch'

Chapter 4

Cream of the Crop

The 1960s was a time of experimentation in the doll world, with manu-facturers vying for sales. Many of them chased gimmicks or, by cutting costs, aimed at the lower end of the market. However, there were some top quality dolls produced, and perhaps three of the best were the range of Sasha dolls manufactured by Frido (later, Trendon), the small Amanda Jane girls and a sturdy little doll known as Babykins, made by Chiltern.

Amanda Jane

To most collectors, the name Amanda Jane conjures up images of a range of small, 8-inch sweet-faced girl dolls, and slightly smaller babies. However, the company did produce other dolls for a while, especially in the 1960s. See Chapter 7 for details of other dolls sold under the Amanda Jane name.

The company was founded in 1952, in London, by Elsin and Conrad Rawnsley, initially for the manufacture of dolls' clothes, to fit dolls of all sizes, but by the late 1950s was marketing a charming hard plastic doll which they called Jinx (see my book *British Dolls of the 1950s*).

In the early 1960s, they moved to an old mill in Petworth, Sussex, where they continued production of the garments and of the Jinx doll. Soon, they were joined by Roy and Peggy Woollett who eventually took control when the Rawnsleys retired. The couple had only been with the company for two years when a dreadful fire ravaged the factory, not only destroying all the stock, but, much more seriously, all the patterns, too, as well as most of the records. The fire was caused by a faulty boiler, and Elsin stated, 'The fire took place because the boiler was not properly installed.' She said that the vents throughout the factory were made from wood, and when huge flames erupted from the oil heater, it was a devastating combination.

Amanda Jane and Jinny (see Chapter 7 for Jinny)

Elsin was at a meeting in the factory when suddenly an assistant burst into the office, asking how the boiler could be turned off as there was a problem. It was too late. As smoke and flames poured out, Elsin rushed the staff to safety. Luckily, everyone was saved. Though the patterns and stock were gone, she most regretted the loss of her Singer sewing machine on which she had designed everything. It had been with her from the very early company beginnings and was of great sentimental value.

Incredibly, although it must have been heartbreaking to see everything, literally, go up in smoke, the company found the strength and resources to start again from scratch. Many decisions were taken, one of the most

Amanda Jane

important being that most of the ranges of dolls' clothing and accessories would be discontinued, and instead the Amanda Jane company would concentrate on the production of a small girl doll, similar to Jinx. Says Peggy Woollett, 'It was decided to concentrate the company's skills on the little 8-inch doll, which from this time onwards was named Amanda Jane.'

Eventually, all was rebuilt, and the garments for the dolls were henceforth designed by Peggy, rather than Elsin, who had now retired.

Incredibly, there was yet another trauma to be weathered – just when everything was running smoothly again, the nearby river burst its banks. Once more, much of the stock was lost, as the mill was flooded to a depth of several feet. Yet the company still soldiered on.

Still very sought after today are the first, 1960s' series of small Amanda Jane girl dolls with large round eyes. Distinctive, and clearly marked with their name, these dolls can be mistaken for no others, and they proved extremely popular with children, but today it is collectors who seek them out. In 1974, the heads were updated and given painted eyes.

An In-Depth Look At An Amanda Jane Sleep-eyed Girl

This delightful little girl stands 7½ inches tall, and is made from vinyl, as opposed to the hard plastic of the Jinx doll, on which she was based.

Amanda Jane

According to Peggy Woollett, 'The original design of the Jinx doll was used as the basis for the Amanda Jane doll, which the company itself started to produce in its purpose-built factory after the fire. The arms, legs, body and head were rotary cast in vinyl.' The doll was originally produced in the Amanda Jane factory in Sussex, using a machine purchased from ICI. In 1968, the production was switched to blow-moulding, and the doll given a polythene body, vinyl head and limbs. This technique significantly increased the doll output.

Her most distinctive features are her eyes – eyes size varies, as does colour. The sleep-eyes' colours include dark brown, light blue, hazel, amber, bright blue, grey and dark blue. These eyes were made by

Amanda Jane

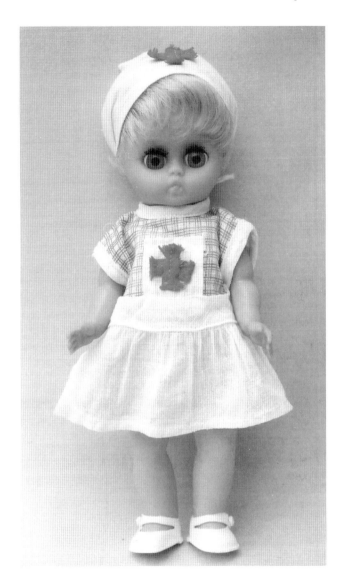

Myers and Parson, of Dalston. She has a small pursed mouth, often painted light pink, which gives her a rather pensive expression. Her lashes are long and her rooted hair is short and silky. The hair was imported for the doll from Germany, and could be obtained in a selection of shades, though most popular seems to have been varying shades of blonde. There is no mistaking this doll for any other as her back is clearly marked 'Amanda Jane. Made in England'. Sometimes, though, sleep-eyed Amanda Jane

Amanda Jane

dolls are found marked 'Hong Kong' – these are not necessarily fakes, as collectors once thought, as it seems a few of the later sleep-eyed dolls were manufactured in Hong Kong, and boxed examples occasionally turn up to prove it.

Amanda Jane is jointed at the neck, shoulders and hips, and her body is that of a child with a slightly plump tummy. Unlike many of the other small dolls of the time, who were still constructed from hard plastic, Amanda Jane's vinyl head meant the doll had combable hair, rather than a wig which would soon fall out or go thin. Consequently she was very popular, especially amongst schoolgirls as she fitted easily into a pocket or satchel, and stood up well to everyday knocks and bumps.

The most exciting thing about this little doll was her range of costumes, which were very up-to-date and featured all the new trends, while still including traditional themes, such as schoolgirl, ballet, Brownie and horse-riding. One of the best-selling items in the 1960s was a print dress made from Liberty lawn trimmed with white lace. Her clothes are easy to recognise, as they bear Amanda Jane name tags. More general garments included a shiny PVC mac, an anorak, a brightly-coloured trouser suit, check pyjamas and a dressing-gown which came with a miniature hot-water bottle. Many of the costumes included a leaflet, with a checklist, enabling young collectors to tick off items as they obtained them. It was pointed out that 'Many of Amanda Jane's outfits are made from fashion fabrics and therefore colours and designs are subject to availability.' This explains the variations found in some outfits (see Chapter 8).

All the intricately-sewn garments were made in Britain (in fact, the company is still in existence and the garments are still created in this country), using talented outworkers. Often the clothes were lined, and they incorporated miniature buckles, buttons, trims, tucks and motifs, as well as real pockets and proper collars and cuffs. The hats worn by the schoolgirl and pony-rider were made using old presses, formed on a cast iron hat block, out of plaster hat moulds. Peggy Woollett explains, 'These are made on our own premises by using traditional Luton hat presses – as were used to make blocked adult hats. The presses we still have could well now be antique, since they were old when we purchased them well over fifty years ago!'

The doll's plastic shoes were either tiny 'Cinderella' brand shoes, or were Amanda Jane own brand types, and they came in a vast range of colours.

Chiltern

As with many doll companies, the story of Chiltern dolls is rather involved. The central character was Leon Rees, a Bavarian gentleman who arrived in London in the 1900s to work at Eisenmann and Company. This company was a major toy importer with branches in Germany and England, and traded under the name 'Einco'. Leon Rees seems to have been a dynamic force, as he worked his way up to become a partner in the concern, and even ended up marrying the boss's daughter.

In 1908, Eisenmann decided to open a subsidiary factory for the production of dolls and this was situated in Chesham, Buckinghamshire, a town deep in the Chiltern hills. Later, the concern expanded to include soft toys.

Babykins by Chiltern

Leon Rees inherited this factory in 1919 when Joseph Eisenmann died, and he went into partnership with Harry Stone, formerly of J.K. Farnell, manufacturers of teddy bears and high-quality plush dolls, to make china-headed and rubber dolls. The pair developed H.G. Stone and Company, opening a factory in North London, and used the brand name 'Chiltern'. Chiltern became renowned for the quality of its products, both dolls and teddy bears, which Eisenmann had begun making in 1915. Today, its most successful teddy bear, the Chiltern Hugmee, dating from the late 1920s, is immensely sought after by teddy enthusiasts. This bear, with its flatter face and wide-eyed look, is very endearing and has become a classic.

Just after the Second World War, Leon Rees and Co. Ltd. became concessionaires for Rosebud dolls, made by Nene plastics, and they sold some of the 7-inch hard plastic types using the Chiltern name. A decade later, the H.G. Stone company moved to Pontypool, Wales, manufacturing vinyl dolls under the Chiltern trademark. Chiltern vinyl dolls soon gained an excellent reputation for the exceptional quality, not only of the design, but also of the vinyl used in the manufacture. Chiltern dolls are much heavier than comparable dolls by other makers, and have a noticeable smoothness of the plastic. Leon Rees died in 1963, and the companies were taken over by the Dunbee-Combex group. Later, they became a division of Chad Valley, which was itself taken over years later.

The Chiltern Babykins was an attempt to make a realistic baby doll, and was heavy, made from a top-quality vinyl, and was modelled to show wrinkles and creases. She had a distinctive posture with a lightly rounded back and down-turned head. Her rather sad face gave the appearance that she would suddenly cry.

An In-Depth Look At A Chiltern Babykins

The Chiltern Babykins, first issued in 1962, was something rather new in the doll world – in fact, she was almost a revolution. At a time when the shops were full of beautiful dolls with smooth faces and long hair, this baby was like a cuckoo in the nest. Her creased and crumpled face, with an expression described by some collectors as 'a bulldog chewing a wasp' or as 'an ugly changeling child', was distinctive and unlike any other doll around at that time. Yet somehow she had an appeal all of her own, and her excellent quality, as well as her unusual appearance endeared her to thousands of children. Nowadays, many collectors seek out Chiltern Babykins dolls, often forming quite large groups, because the babies all seem to vary.

Babykins came in two sizes, 15 inches and 19 inches, and featured a variety of short hair styles – sometimes there were just a few wisps, while occasionally there was a mop of curls. A close look at this doll reveals her strange posture – her head looks down rather than the usual eyes forward position, it seems particularly noticeable in the larger size of doll; it is almost as if the Chiltern designer thought he was designing hump-backed teddy bears once more. I wondered about this for some time, till suddenly every-thing fell, literally, into place. The Babykins was designed to lie down just as a new baby would. If she is placed in a cot or pram, her head is held at exactly the correct angle, unlike the majority of dolls who, once reclining, tend to stare uncomfortably upwards. She is a masterpiece of design and originality.

Babykins by Chiltern

**Babykins by
Chiltern**

This baby is obviously a well-nourished child, with plump cheeks and podgy limbs. She has sleep-eyes, long lashes and high, arched eyebrows which give her a slightly quizzical air. Her eye colour varies; many are deep blue or grey, but one of my favourites has black, velvety 'pansy' eyes, which are most unusual. Babykins' nose is tip-tilted and small, and her mouth is moulded to reveal her tongue which adds to the sweet, inno-cent babylike expression. The lips are painted red, and two small creases run downwards from each corner, while a tiny fold above her receding chin is a cute touch. Most often found are honey-blondes, though dark blondes do turn up, as do brunettes. There are also black versions of the doll, with black hair. It is interesting to note that under the hair, curls are marked out in the vinyl – this practice was regularly found on hard plastic dolls of the previous decade, which were prone to losing their wigs, but it seems odd to find a doll with rooted hair similarly marked. Collectors sometimes worry that the doll has had her hair chopped by a young would-be hairdresser, but many of these Chiltern Babykins were purposely sold with a short, irregular cut or a chopped-off 'pudding basin' style.

The modelling of her fingers is superb, with those on the right hand curled inwards. The thumb on the left hand is angled just right for her to suck. Both arms are bent, as are the legs, with their delightfully chubby knees. Markings on this doll vary; the earlier models are marked HG Stone, others Chiltern, while some are unmarked. It is likely that these unmarked dolls were sold through various chain stores.

When the dolls were sold, they could be found wearing either a pretty, traditional style baby frock made from nylon, or a romper-suit. They could also be bought undressed, as was customary at the time, when knitting and dressmaking were still popular pastimes. The Museum of Childhood at Bethnal Green was so impressed with the Chiltern Babykins, that they immediately included one amongst their exhibits, as an example of a well-designed English doll.

The Chiltern company produced a range of dolls of all kinds, from babies to teens, but none so memorable as Babykins. They include a cheeky baby with an asymmetrical smile, a soft-bodied baby and even a doll-shaped nightdress case (see Chapter 6).

Sasha

Of all the play dolls, it must be the Sasha range which bridged the gulf between dolls and sculpture. Sasha dolls, with their quiet understated features and their smooth jointing were true artists' dolls – really, much too good for children to play with!

Frido/Trendon

The Sasha story begins with a Swiss artist, Sasha Morgenthaler, who was born in 1893, later studying art and sculpture. One of her projects was a range of playing cards depicting various animals. At first they were hand-drawn and coloured, but later became mass-produced. Sasha decided she wanted to create a doll, as she was unhappy with the design of the dolls sold at the time, and during the 1940s began experimenting with various sculpts. Her aim was to produce a doll which not only would resemble a real child, but which would appeal to those from all cultures. The dolls which she made are known to today's collectors as 'Studio Sculpts', and change hands for enormous amounts of money.

A Sasha face means different things to different people – it registers emotions. Children liked the dolls because they gave rein to the imagination – the doll could be happy, sad, thoughtful or mischie-

Sasha 1967 redhead by Frido/Trendon

vous. Sasha aimed for asymmetry, just like the human face, to give her dolls a true human expression. It seems that Sasha placed great importance on the doll's eyes, painting them only after the doll was almost complete, and when she finally allowed them to go into mass production, was particularly strict about the eye painting.

When, at last, she decided that her dolls should reach a wider market – making them by hand was extremely time-consuming, and the cost meant she could only sell at high prices – she approached the German company, Gotz Puppenfabrik, knowing that, to be affordable to all, it was necessary to have the dolls factory-made. The Gotz company began manufacturing them in 1964, and not long after, John and Sara Doggart of the Frido company, later Trendon, of Stockport, England, were given the licence to make the dolls too, producing their first Sashas in time for the 1966 British Toy Fair. Trendon continued to make the dolls in the UK until 1986, though Gotz ceased making them sixteen years earlier.

Frido (who often used the name Frida) were manufacturers of plastic balls – it was their main claim to fame. In fact, their 1963 Doll Catalogue boasted in large letters on the front cover, 'Frida Dolls are made by Frido Ltd, manufacturers of the famous vinyl balls'. The dolls which the company produced at this time were pretty, attractive but of no special importance (see Chapter 7). All this was to change with the arrival of Sasha.

The company was based in Reddish, Stockport, in an old mill, and was part of the Friedland group, who are still renowned today for their various door chimes. Frido was known in the early 1960s as a general toy and doll manufacturer, but when John Doggart took over on the death of the Director, he and his wife decided to look for some more 'up-market' dolls to produce. After seeing photos of Sasha Morgenthaler's dolls in *Graphis*, they contacted her and the rest is history. Sasha Morgenthaler died in 1975, aged eighty-two, but her legacy lives on.

AN IN-DEPTH LOOK AT A SASHA DOLL

When the first English Sasha dolls were produced in 1966, they looked slightly different to the later versions. The main difference was the lack of a philtrum, the two small lines which run from the nose to the lips. By 1968, a philtrum was added, and the dolls, although still with subtle variations, basically stayed the same until they ceased production.

Sasha stands 16 inches tall, (earliest dolls are 15½ inches, later dolls 17

Sasha 1967 in gingham by Frido/Trendon

Gregor 1968 by Frido/Trendon

inches), and is made from a smooth, hard pale-milk-chocolate coloured vinyl which is very tactile. Her face is gently rounded, her eyes are painted – at first they were hand-finished over a sprayed guideline – and her lips are lightly coloured. Her skin is free from wrinkles and creases; she is un-ruffled and flawless! Her hair is thickly rooted, and is long and lustrous.

Her body is asymmetrical, and is jointed at neck, hips and shoulders. These parts are strung with thick elastic cord, the colours of which give collectors a clue to the year of production. The asymmetry, coupled with the strong elastic, allows the doll to assume many different, natural poses. Her left arm is slightly curved, with her bent fingers facing downwards, while her right arm is bent and the fingers and hand curve towards her body. Due to the method of construction, the arms will stay where they are placed. The doll can stand up by herself. She bears no marks (unlike the Gotz version).

Sasha dolls were quality examples; the kind of special doll a child might be given by doting grandparents, or by parents who were confident their child would not mishandle it. They were relatively expensive, even in their heyday, and today are sought by collectors, especially the earlier versions.

There were three main types produced by the Frido/Trendon factory – Sasha (girl), Gregor (boy) and baby dolls. The babies were 12 inches tall, and featured bent legs as opposed to the straight ones of the girls and boys. The dolls can be further classed by colour – black, dark brown or pale (the classic shade) – and by hair colour of blonde, brunette, honey-blonde or redhead. The babies can be sexed or unsexed. A couple of the later versions of the dolls came with wigs, rather than rooted hair. In addition, there was a toddler doll ready to go into production just before Trendon ceased production. A few types of toddlers (babies with straight legs) were, however, made in the 1990s by the Gotz company in Germany. Cora and Caleb, the black girl and boy, and also the babies, didn't appear until the 1970s.

Just as much care was taken with the outfits of the Sasha dolls; considering the range and span of the issue of Sasha, Gregor and babies, the designs were surprisingly limited when compared to other dolls from other manufacturers. The most popular outfit in Britain was the blue gingham dress; a simple, long-sleeved dress, quite short, made from soft brushed cotton and which fastened at the back with two poppers (later Velcro). Two further poppers fastened the cuffs. The dress had a high yoke, and a white rounded Peter Pan collar. This blue and white dress first appeared in 1965, and was still in use when Sasha dolls were finally discontinued in 1985.

Amongst the other 1960s' Sasha outfits were a pale pink drop-waist party frock, a white jumper and red kilt, a white ballet outfit with a tartan cape, dungarees and top, and a navy-blue or brown long-sleeved corduroy dress. Gregor was sold in denim jeans and a navy jumper, short trousers and a white shirt, or pyjamas and a red dressing-gown. A red duffel coat was available separately. At this time, the dolls wore red or white leather shoes in various styles, including ankle-strap, slip-on and sandals. When sold, each doll wore a small metal seal on a thin cord around their wrist.

Chapter 5

Tiny Tears

The Tiny Tears doll was probably Palitoy's greatest triumph – certainly, she won many awards and was every little girl's must-have by the late 1960s. After her introduction in 1965, Palitoy continued to make her for twenty years, before eventually she was passed on to other manufacturers. Amazingly, she is still in production today, an unbroken run of almost forty-five years. Initially, she was made at the Palitoy factory in Coalville, Leicestershire.

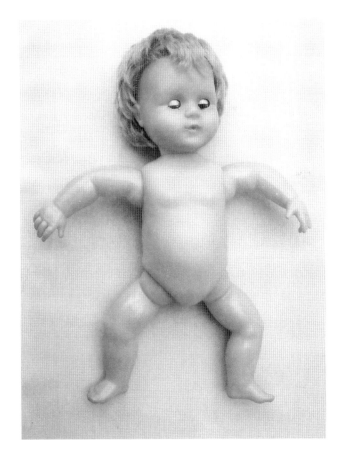

Tiny Tears by Palitoy, showing the ball-jointed limbs

The doll broke new ground in doll design – to begin with, she featured innovative ball-jointing which meant that, when she was picked up and cradled in a child's arms, she would flop, just like a real baby. This distinctive jointing makes her easily recognisable to today's doll collectors and mint or all-original dolls are very much in demand.

Small girls adored Tiny Tears, learning about her through a major advertising campaign, and they instantly took her to their hearts. She not only looked like a baby, she handled like one, too; she was cuddly and dainty. Best of all, she performed the three basic baby functions – she could drink from a bottle, cry real tears, and wet her nappy. Tiny Tears' faces were hand-painted, which accounts for the tremendous variation in colour and detail.

The ball-jointing was designed by Stuart Moore, who also sculpted the face of the doll. He had worked at Cascelloid (who used the Palitoy tradename) for ten years and was an experienced designer. Stuart modelled the head from clay before taking a wax casting. From this was made the metal mould, and then the doll was cast in vinyl. Tiny Tears dolls were made using the rotational moulding method and were originally cast in two halves. The Americans had already been using the name 'Tiny Tears' since 1950, but their doll didn't have the ball-joints and the face was completely different to the British version. More baby-like than the British doll, the American Tiny Tears cried, drank and blew bubbles through a pipe.

The first British Tiny Tears doll made her debut at the British Toy Fair in 1964, and won the award for the best Girls' Toy of the Year. She went on to win the award twice more. Tiny Tears cost 53/11 (£2.70) in the mid-1960s.

AN IN-DEPTH LOOK AT A TINY TEARS DOLL

This is the first British Tiny Tears doll, issued in 1965. She is 16 inches high, a perfect size for a child to hold, and is marked '16D Made in England' on the back of her neck. Sometimes this number can also be found at the top of the limbs. She has bent arms and legs, and her delicate fingers are beautifully modelled. Her revolutionary ball-joints, or, as collectors refer to them, rotational joints, allow her limbs to flop naturally and realistically. There is a waxy sheen to the vinyl, a feature of many of

Tiny Tears by Palitoy, blue gingham version

the early Tiny Tears dolls. Often, these early versions have seam lines down the body and the limbs, but these were removed during one of the body remoulds, so they aren't seen on later dolls. Also, the first Tiny Tears, as well as many of the 1970s' dolls, don't have navels; this feature was later introduced on one of the body remoulds.

This Tiny Tears has a slim face with blue sleeping-eyes and long 'real' lashes, as well as additional lower lashes painted on. Her small open mouth is just large enough to take the plastic teat of a bottle. She has fine, sparse blonde hair which feels soft, just like a baby's. No dark-haired dolls were issued at this time, while black versions didn't appear until the 1980s. Not only is she comfortable to cuddle, she can be safely bathed, and her rooted hair can be shampooed, brushed and combed without fear of it falling out.

She is wearing her original outfit of a fine-checked gingham romper which fastens with two white poppers at the back and three between the legs. This romper was available in rose pink or mid blue, and was edged with white cotton lace around the leg openings. This was the only outfit actually sold on the first model, though other items of clothing could be purchased separately. Tiny Tears also wears a towelling bib with a pink or blue teardrop logo – these bibs are hard to find nowadays, especially with the logos intact, as they tended to run when washed and so no doubt the majority were thrown away.

When she was sold, she came with a small plastic feeding bottle, a plastic dummy or 'soother', and an instruction leaflet explaining how to make Tiny Tears cry.

This instruction leaflet reads:

1 Remove soother from Tiny Tears' mouth.
2 Fill the feeding bottle with clean water.
3 Insert nozzle of feeding bottle into Tiny Tears' mouth.
4 Squeeze bottle until Tiny Tears has 'drunk' all the water.
5 Replace soother in mouth and firmly squeeze tummy several times.
6 LOOK! Tiny Tears is crying real tears! (And nappy-wetting too. Perhaps that explains the tears. Wipe them away, change the nappy, and Tiny Tears will feel better again.)

These instructions, with slight variations, continued right through the Palitoy years. In 1970, the doll was remodelled, appearing briefly with a

Early Tiny Tears' leaflet

Tiny Tears by Palitoy, pink gingham version

strange, squashed look to her face, and seeming much older. Nowadays collectors refer to these as Transitionals. In 1972, the doll was revamped again, appearing with thick yellow hair and looking more like a small child. The daintiness of the very first Tiny Tears had been lost.

Doll collector Sharon White recounts, 'There is one doll which will always hold an extra special place in my heart and that is the very first "Tiny Tears" made in 1965. I was lucky enough to be given one for my birthday in 1966 (I think!) and I thought she was just wonderful! She went everywhere with me and there was nothing I liked better than feeding her water in her bottle and then watching the tears fall from her eyes and her nappy get very wet when I squeezed her tummy – it's no wonder she cried when I think of the force used on that poor tummy!

'Anyway, one sunny summer's day I was playing with her in the garden as usual, sat in my little wicker chair happily feeding her, when I was aware that my dad had arrived with his ciné camera at the ready to film me in

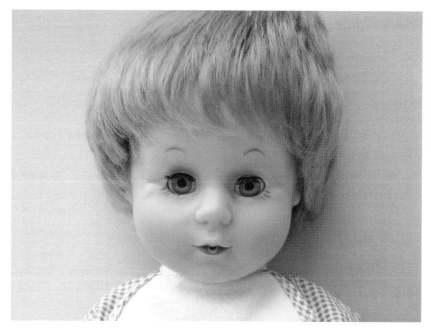

Tiny Tears by Palitoy

action. Always one to play to the camera, I cheerfully obliged, going through the ritual as normal of feeding, pressing her tummy, taking all her clothes off and changing her. You can imagine my total horror, then, on taking her nappy off to find it a nasty dark yellow colour inside – my dad had thought it would be great fun to fill her nappy with mustard and then watch my face while he filmed me!! It's all preserved for posterity, and you could guarantee that every couple of years at Christmas time when my dad would decide to show his ciné films, out would come that one!

'My original Tiny Tears had long ago been given away and I always wanted to find another just like her, but was resigned to the fact I probably never would, when along came eBay and I found my special doll all over again! The only thing I don't have for her is her original bottle, but I'm sure I'll find one in time and then I'll just have to hope that my husband doesn't decide he wants to fill her nappy with mustard . . .'

Teeny Tiny Tears

In 1967 Palitoy decided that Tiny Tears should have a younger sister, and so Teeny Tiny Tears came into being. Facially, she resembled her big sister with the same blue eyes, open mouth and wispy hair, but at 12 inches, was much smaller – she was a perfect size for the younger child. Teeny Tiny Tears featured the same rotational limbs and drink and wet mechanism as that of Tiny Tears, but her hands were differently moulded; they were slightly more curved and her thumb could be made to go into her mouth, though it wouldn't stay there for long. She was marked '12B Made in England' on the back of the neck.

This pretty doll was dressed in a pink or pale blue nylon gingham dress with a frilled hem over a ribbon-tied nappy. It fastened at the back with two white poppers. Her small white bib bore a pink or blue floral motif

Teeny Tiny Tears by Palitoy

and was edged with white cotton braid. Just like her older sister, she came with a feeding bottle and dummy.

Teeny Tiny Tears was updated in 1970, together with her sister, and given thicker hair, a rounder face and an older look. This doll was eventually discontinued in 1982, and by then she had an even smaller sister.

Outfits and Accessories

Palitoy Tiny Tears was sold with a bottle and a dummy, as was Teeny Tiny Tears. The tiny dummies were about an inch and a quarter long, with a ring through which a ribbon could be looped, but it's probable most chil-

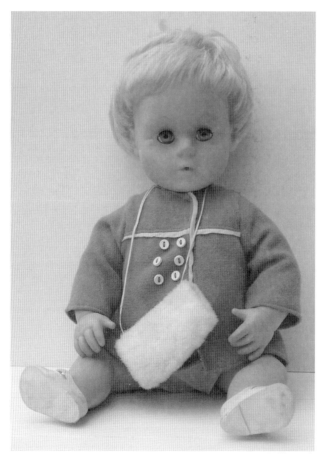

Tiny Tears in 'Winter Baby' coat

dren didn't bother with ribbon – no doubt, hundreds of the dummies were sucked up by the vacuum cleaner, lost down cracks in floorboards, or worse, swallowed by children! 'Tiny Tears' was written in script on the disc of the dummy, so they are easy to identify today. Over the years they came in various colours including white, pink and light brown.

Feeding bottles were two-and-a-half inches long, and were made from an opaque white soft plastic. Each bottle was carefully embossed with calibration lines/numbers, just like a real baby's bottle of the time. The pink teat-shaped top was made from a harder plastic, and was fixed in place. To fill the bottle with water, it was necessary to immerse it, then squeeze to create a vacuum causing the bottle to fill. Unlike the dummies, they were unmarked.

A selection of clothing was sold separately for the 1960s' Tiny Tears and Teeny Tears, and included party dresses, nightwear and romper-suits. Amongst the earliest outfits for Tiny Tears were 'Playtime' (sleeveless smock and trousers), 'Clean Baby' (waterproof smock, knickers, nappies), 'Winter Baby' (coat with six buttons, hat and muff), 'Sunday Best' (ribbon-trimmed dress and booties) and 'Sleepy Baby' (nightdress which converted into a sleeping bag). Teeny Tiny Tears had similar outfits, though there were minor changes. The greatest difference was in 'Playtime', where Teeny's outfit was a short smock, pants and bonnet. The outfits were packaged up with a bottle and dummy. Gradually the range increased, to include christening dresses, cotton frocks and romper-suits. Sadly, they were all unlabelled, making it very difficult to identify many of the outfits with any degree of certainty.

By 1969, outfits included 'Beddie Byes' (embroidered nightdress which converted into sleeping bag), 'Warm and Cosy' (double-breasted coat and hat), 'Birthday Girl' (gingham dress and knickers), 'Tea Time' (pretty overall and 'knix') and 'Playhour' (romper-suit and bib). Similar outfits were sold for Teeny Tiny Tears.

The 1969 *Which?* Report

A fascinating report was published in the consumer magazine, *Which?*, in November 1969, comparing various dolls and outfits. Amongst those chosen were Tiny Tears and her sister Teeny Tiny Tears. Both dolls were heavily criticised, but the report makes very interesting reading. (The Tiny Tears tested was the first Palitoy version in the check romper-suit and bib, while the Teeny Tiny Tears was the gingham dress version.)

At that time the price of Tiny Tears was £3.2s 6d (£3.13) – so had already increased significantly from the 53/11 (£2.69) quoted earlier. Teeny Tiny Tears was £2.9s 11d. The magazine explained that there were five identical outfits for each doll sold separately, costing from 19s 11d (99p) to 27s 6d (£1.37) for Tiny Tears, and from 16s 11d (85p) to 24s 9d (£1.24) for Teeny Tiny Tears. A dummy and bottle were supplied with every outfit.

Which? described the clothing as: 'Generally simple baby clothes. Quality of materials fair; finish and workmanship fair to good. Some clothes fraying… Some dresses too short and nappies impossible to fit properly. Clothes fit well to very well – though some outfits gaped at back.' The report also mentioned that the colour ran on nearly every outfit causing stains, that some clothes shrank a lot, and that the dolls' hair washed badly and was inclined to stand on end. However, they presented no safety hazards, and though they could burn, as soon as the flame was removed they went out. Today's collectors might well want to heed the remarks about clothing washability.

This *Which?* report compared a selection of dolls with Tiny Tears,

Tiny Tears bib – these tend to fade and run when wet

including Amanda Jane, Sasha, Gregor, Barbie, Sindy, Tressy, Palitoy's Goldilocks and a Pedigree foam-bodied baby called Michele. This last doll was declared the best buy in the baby doll section (see Chapter 6). It is very interesting to note, almost forty years later, that Tiny Tears, Amanda Jane, Barbie and Sindy are all still made today, while Sasha was discontinued only recently. The best buy, Pedigree's Michele, was only in the shops for a few years, before sinking without trace!

Tiny Tears in a Tri-ang pushchair

Chapter 6

Major Companies

Thousands of dolls were issued in the 1960s; some went on to become classics, while others fell by the wayside, or were popular for a short while but didn't have enough 'oomph' to ensure they would be long-remembered. Here are some of the dolls sold by major companies at the time.

Chiltern

Chiltern dolls are renowned by collectors for the quality and weight of the vinyl. Although they were only in production for around ten years, the numerous dolls found in such good condition bear testimony to the superiority of the materials used (see Chapter 4).

Unfortunately, many years after the company had closed, a batch of dolls appeared on the market which were marked 'Chiltern' on the back of the neck but were clearly of a lesser quality. These dolls were very lightweight, and were of a very bright shade of pink. I don't believe these were intentional 'fakes' as such; the moulds had obviously been sold on to another factory, probably in the Far East, who, quite legitimately, had used them to produce dolls. Obviously, they should have removed the trademark, but it is more than likely they didn't realise the significance. It is, though, just as well to be aware that these dolls are around – once they have been handled, the difference in quality is easy to spot.

In Chapter 4 we looked at the Babykins doll, a classic of design and moulding, which is still very much collected today. These sturdy dolls stood up well to the constant rough and tumble of childhood play.

Many Chiltern dolls had character-type faces rather than traditionally pretty dolly-faces, but they were still cute, not ugly as so many character faces can be. There were beauties too, of course, with big blue eyes, beautiful hair and bright red cupid's-bow lips. A cute, character baby, just 10

Chiltern girl doll

inches high, featured a very unusual asymmetrical smile. This cheeky-faced doll had a much more natural expression than that normally worn by baby dolls at the time, and was crowned with a crop of curly Saran hair. Today, doll enthusiasts refer to him as a Chiltern Cheeky. He dates from 1964, and has a twin sister whose hair is a little longer. Though usually dark blonde, sometimes brunettes or redheads turn up. For a while, the Chiltern Cheeky dolls were featured in *Woman's Weekly*, which created all kinds of patterns for them – people still had time to make dolls' clothes in the 1960s. Sometimes collectors come across a similar doll bearing the mark of an Italian company, so presumably the moulds of this doll, too, were sold off when the company closed.

Collector Lesley Glover from the Isle of Wight found a beautiful Chiltern girl, 'Debbie'. She says, 'Debbie is 12 inches high and made from heavy duty vinyl. She is marked "Chiltern Made in England" on her neck.

**Chiltern
Cheeky**

Her hair is set in a mass of curls and she has open and closing dark blue glassine eyes. I don't think her dress is original as these dolls were popularised in the women's magazines of the mid 1960s and were offered, undressed, by mail order from Messrs. Bentalls Ltd. Toy Department, Kingston-upon-Thames, Surrey for 19s 11d plus 2s 6d p&p extra if you lived outside London. There were a whole series of knitting patterns for her, such as "Doll Tourist in Paris" (dress and tammy with pom-pom), "Little Red Riding Hood" (dress and cape), "For a Well Dressed Miss" (coat and dress), "Sleepyhead" (frilled nightdress), "And so to Bed" (night-

Chiltern
'Debbie'

gown and dressing-gown), "Model in Miniature" (two-piece, coat, full set of underwear), "Dolly Mixtures" (delightful outfits for Debbie, trouser suit and dress). This particular doll has her swing ticket, receipt and her Bentalls' paper bag stating she was bought on December 10th and cost 19s 11d. A Christmas present, no doubt, for some lucky little girl.'

Particularly sweet was a 16½-inch soft-bodied doll with sleep-eyes, very short hair and clenched fists. She featured a cute rounded chin, and had

Chiltern soft-bodied baby

been modelled in such a way that when she was laid down, her arms went up to her ears, just the way a young baby often sleeps. The range of girl dolls was attractive, and, once again, their hands are noteworthy, with excellent modelling. Their faces, though pretty, are often animated, such as a 13½-inch high bent-leg girl from the early 1960s with thick, honey-blonde rooted hair and large blue eyes. Straight-legged dolls were made too, including 'Carol', a 17-inch girl dating from 1967 with waist-length shiny rooted nylon hair, and wearing a short yellow braid-trimmed smock, red tights and black shoes, retailing at 45/9 (£2.29), and 'Patricia', with long blonde hair, dressed in a pretty needlecord dress with puffed sleeves, slightly dearer at 50/9 (£2.53). The company also seem to have shared some moulds with Frido (see Chapter 7), as some of their dolls have identical faces.

Chiltern advertised smaller dolls too, including Melissa, 13 inches high. She was fully jointed, with her arms slightly splayed to the side and fingers wide (similar to Debbie). Melissa's hair reached to her waist and was held back from her face by a wide ribbon. She cost 35/6 (£1.78). There was also a selection of teens in various sizes available, from 11 inches to 20 inches tall. Many of these were extremely sophisticated, with posh full-skirted evening dresses and fur stoles, while others wore everyday cotton frocks (see Chapter 2).

Chiltern girl doll

Chiltern made sure that their dolls showed up well in toyshops, by packing them in distinctive rose-pink boxes bearing the delightful slogan 'A Chiltern doll goes straight to a little girl's heart'. In 1967 the Chiltern company became a subsidiary of Chad Valley.

Palitoy

A huge range of dolls poured forth from this company's Coalville factory, in Leicestershire. Its most famous creation was probably Tiny Tears, (see

Nurse Carol by Palitoy

Chapter 5) but there were many other attractive, well-made dolls. The company sent shock waves throughout Britain in 1966 when it began producing Action Man – parents had to adjust to the fact that it was okay to give a boy a doll!

It's impossible to list all the dolls which appeared courtesy of Palitoy during the 1960s, and although emphasis seems to have been, at least from the mid-sixties, on Tiny Tears and her range, other dolls included Goldilocks, Pouting Pretti, Walk 'n' Talk Poppet, Dolly Darlings, Pretty Miss Kiss, Pennies and Nurse Carol, as well as a selection of mechanical dolls (see Chapter 9).

Nurse Carol was a particularly delightful doll dating from the early 1960s. The teen type doll wore a nurse's uniform of the time – dark blue dress, white apron, red belt, black stockings and white cap. She was vinyl with rooted hair, stood 15 inches high and her feet were arched to take high-heeled shoes. Her arms were bent, and cradled in them were two tiny twin babies; obviously she was en route to show the twins to the proud father! Lesley Glover, a nurse from the Isle of Wight who owns one of these dolls, remarks, 'On the edge of the box it says the doll's name is Nurse Carol and the catalogue number is 3776. Nurse Carol is totally unmarked but her two 3-inch hard plastic babies are marked "Made in England" across their backs. Interestingly Nurse Carol wears a lovely bra and pants, seamed hold-up black stockings and HIGH heels. Can't imagine doing my job wearing these!!'

Lesley also has some Palitoy dolls representing older girls, though, unlike the teens, they don't have arched feet and high heels. These girls wear basic flat plastic shoes. She believes the dolls are called Sarah and date from 1965, adding, 'They are 18 inches high, made from heavy vinyl, and with "18c Made in England" in a line on their necks. The dolls have lovely faces and washable hair, and an indication of a teen body shape. Their eyes have blue/green eyeshadow and their lower lashes are painted. I think they're wearing their original dresses, they are both dressed in striped material.'

Pouting Pretti was a 12-inch high baby wearing a yellow sleepsuit and hat. Her face was made of a rubbery 'skin' over an armature, which allowed the doll to change her expression from a pout to a smile. She had painted eyes and a slightly strange face due to the armature. To change the expression it was necessary to move the doll's arm. She cost 34/11 (£1.74)

**Pretty Miss Kiss
by Palitoy**

in the late sixties, and was very similar to dolls by other companies, including Pedigree's 'Baby Sparkle Eyes' (though the Pedigree doll was almost twice the price of the Palitoy version) and 'Baby Tickle Tears' from Deluxe Reading.

A much more conventional doll was Walk 'n' Talk Poppet, who featured a mass of cascading blonde hair, and was dressed 'Victorian style' in a broderie anglaise smock over a long-sleeved dress. Walk 'n' Talk Poppet, 23 inches tall, had a repertoire of eleven sayings. She was a pricey doll, costing 127/9 (£6.39) in 1967. Pretty Miss Kiss was an 18-inch doll, whose slightly pouting mouth gave a clue to her name. When her arm was squeezed, she 'blew a kiss'. She wore a nautical style outfit, in red or blue and had blue eyes. Her blonde hair was styled in plaits.

The Goldilocks series of hair-grow dolls made their debut in the late sixties. Of the same ilk as Tressy, Goldilocks too was a 'grow hair' type.

Goldilocks by Palitoy

Dolly Darlings by Palitoy, 'School Days'

However, she was much taller than Tressy, standing 15 inches high, and she proved to be a great favourite due to her magic hair. Her head and arms were soft vinyl, her body and legs were harder, and she was marked 'AP 15 Made in England'. Goldilocks had blue eyes and a rather serious face. Her hair, of course, was blonde, with a thick growing strand protruding from a hole in the top of her head, the length of which could be controlled by turning a large knob in her back or pressing a button in her tummy. Goldilocks was issued by Palitoy in 1968, and was sold in a variety of ultra-short outfits, as was the fashion. The first doll in the series was dressed in a blue denim skirt which featured two large orange daisies, (daisies, especially with rounded petals, were very much in vogue in the sixties), denim knickers and an orange blouse.

Other costumes were available to buy separately. She was updated in the early 1970s, and given a slightly different face with more of a smile. This attractive Goldilocks girl was advertised as 'The doll with 101 hairstyles' – although the leaflet only showed six, according to the *Which?* magazine survey of 1969! *Which?* remarked that the hair washed quite well, though 'went on to lose some of its curling', and that the flower trims on the blue and orange dress tended to run in the wash. They concluded 'Her outfits were fairly good and she was much the better of the two growing hair dolls' (the other was Tressy). The magazine went on to say that they thought her good value. At that time, Goldilocks was priced at £2.14.11 (£2.75). She was a popular young lady – it was the attraction of the hair which could magically be a short bob, or waist length, just like Tressy! (see Chapter 3).

A favourite series of Palitoy dolls had American connections – Dolly Darlings. These cute little dolls, just over 4 inches tall, date from the mid-1960s, and though marketed by Palitoy in Britain, they originated in the United States. Many of their outfits, such as the 'Go Team Go' dress, have a definite American feel.

The dainty dolls were made from vinyl, and jointed at neck, shoulders and hips, while later models were also jointed at the waist. They had painted side-glance eyes, but their most distinctive feature was the open mouth revealing one tiny tooth. Most of the dolls found in the UK have rooted nylon hair in

Dolly Darlings by Palitoy, 'Tea Time'

various colours, lengths and styles. However, the earliest (US) dolls had moulded hair, although they were virtually identical to the later dolls in outfits and design. Each doll had its arms held out from the sides in a dainty gesture, and was marked 'Hasbro' on the back. There were plenty of variations in hair and eye colour, and so there are often new kinds to be found.

Outfits for Dolly Darlings included 'School Days' – a blue and green tartan skirt with a green top and white blouse; 'Slumber Party' – two-piece turquoise blue pyjamas – and 'Tea Time', which was a sophisticated dress with a black bodice, white net skirt and painted-on short white gloves. 'Go Team Go' consisted of a royal blue shift trimmed with red and the letters DD (presumably standing for Dolly Darlings!), worn over a long-sleeved white top, while 'Boy Trap' was a short peach mini-dress, and

Pennies by Palitoy

'Hipster', a green and purple striped mini with matching hat. 'Summer Day' was a pretty white dress featuring an appliquéd pink daisy and matching headscarf. The dolls were finished off with painted shoes and socks, and the shoe styles varied quite a bit; amongst them were T-bar, strap, slip-ons and slippers. The dolls were on sale in Britain for almost ten years, and are very collectable today.

Doll-lover Shelley Cuff remembers, 'One Christmas my parents had bought me a second-hand doll's house. It was an enormous house, much too big to hide away whilst they were working on it, so it was placed on the table in the front room, tied up in a curtain. I was told that Father Christmas's elves were working on it and that I mustn't peep. Well of

Action Man by Palitoy

Vectis Auctions

course, I couldn't resist, and untied the curtain to have a look. Inside were some Dolly Darling dolls which I proceeded to play with. I had a great time until I accidentally snapped the head off one. I quickly replaced everything and cleared off, out of the room. I can't remember ever being told off so I guess my parents thought the doll was already damaged.'

Another range of small Palitoy dolls was the Pennies series. Pennies were slightly larger than Dolly Darlings, at 6 inches high, and were just as sweet. They are not so easy to find today as they were only made for a short time. As they were not dressed so fashionably, they don't have the same appeal as Dolly Darlings, and are not so collectable. Even so, they have immense charm with their painted black dot eyes, snub noses and gentle smiles. Pennies were sold in small cello-fronted boxes, at easily affordable prices, and their range of outfits sold for, if not pennies, at least pocket money prices.

Action Man was first made by Palitoy under licence from Hasbro in 1966. In the States this action figure was referred to as GI Joe, but in Britain we knew him as Action Man. His arrival must have initially caused many a rugged Dad to sob into his beer at the thought that his son might be a 'cissy', but in fact the wide range of accessories, both military and civilian, which were developed for Action Man led to plenty of creative play. He had a full range of outfits and vehicles, and later became even more sophisticated with 'moving eagle eyes' and a speech mechanism.

The early Action Man had painted, moulded hair rather than the fuzzy type which was introduced in 1970, and was fully poseable. The painted hair was available in four different shades. The first figures were a soldier, a pilot and a sailor, each dressed in basic uniforms complete with dog tags, and the range of accessories, right from the start, was excellent.

Pedigree

Lines Brothers continued to expand, not just in Britain, but abroad as well, and by the 1960s Lines Brothers/Tri-ang/Pedigree could claim to be the 'largest toy empire in the world'. However, the most significant move for British doll-lovers was the opening of a new factory in Canterbury in 1966. This became home to many classic dolls including Sindy and the 70s' very popular Baby First Love. For a while, it seemed as though Pedigree could do no wrong; their dolls were everywhere, and during the 1960s they filled toyshops with thousands of dolls of all shapes and sizes.

Apart from Sindy, other 1960s' Pedigree dolls included Mandy, Tiny Talker – a doll so popular, she was kept in the Pedigree range for several years – Michele, Sparkle Eyes, Talkative Jane, Baby Party, Susie Sing-a-Song and, in the early part of the decade, a range of large teens (see Chapter 2 and Chapter 9). There was also a huge series of baby and girl dolls (and a few boys), many of which, according to the 1966 catalogue, were unnamed. It seems that often, stores and mail order catalogues which sold the dolls made up their own names, as sometimes the same doll appears in several catalogues under various names. Throughout the decade, many of the dolls were sold bearing silver plastic logo badges, reading 'Pedigree' in script, adding an attractive finishing touch to their outfits (as well as making the outfits more easy for collectors to identify decades later!).

Some Pedigree dolls did bear official names, however – Susan, Anne, Eileen, Denise, Barbara, for instance, featured in the 1960s' catalogue – while others just bore general descriptions, such as Ponytail doll, Doll with long hair, Thumb-sucking doll and Bride doll. A range of baby dolls appeared in 1965, made from a particularly sturdy vinyl. These attractive dolls had beautifully modelled fingers and toes, and featured moulded hair. They were perfect for bathing. As with several other companies of the time, Pedigree also featured a range of ultra large girl dolls (termed 'Companion Dolls' in the United States), standing 36 inches high, and a selection of life-size toddlers, 30 inches, all excellently made in quality materials.

Pedigree doll in box, ready to dress

Interestingly, Pedigree were also involved with marketing some of the Chatty Cathy series of dolls which appeared under the Rosebud/Mattel partnership (see Chapter 9). Just as with the last decade, Pedigree, along with most other manufacturers, still sold many dolls undressed, ready to be clothed at home. The company also attempted to introduce a line for boys, presumably after noting the success of GI Joe in America (which was sold here as Action Man, by Palitoy). The Pedigree boys' range was Tommy Gunn, but was fairly short-lived, and was mainly military-themed. An attempt was made in the 1970s to resurrect him, under licence to Zodiac toys, but this did not prove very popular.

Pedigree boy doll

A Tri-ang catalogue dating from the late sixties shows many attractive dolls; the majority are talking or mechanical types (see Chapter 9), as well as 'basic' baby and girl dolls such as Jill, a 22-inch high girl with long brown hair in a fringed style, wearing a short gaily printed smock over a pair of red trews, and Cherry and Victoria, both long-haired blondes, again with thick fringes (fringes were very fashionable at the time!). Cherry was a 17-inch tall walking doll wearing a red felt dress with cherry motifs over a

**Tommy Gunn
by Pedigree**

**Michele by
Pedigree**

broderie anglaise bodice, while Victoria, also 17 inches, had a more old-fashioned look with a dark green plaid dress worn over white stockings. Barbara, a 16-inch baby girl, wore a lemon check nylon dress, and had sleep-eyes and short curly blonde hair. The dolls retailed at between £2.2.6 (£2.13) and £2.15.0 (£2.75).

Michele was a soft-bodied baby with vinyl head, arms and legs, and was issued in the late 1960s. She was quite small at 12 inches, and had short rooted hair in various colours and sleep-eyes. Her closed mouth was modelled in a shy smile, and she had one clenched fist while the other hand was splayed. She was sold dressed in a short blue angel top and matching pants, with her name, 'Michele', printed across the fabric. Pedigree said she was, 'The best little baby in the whole wide world.'

Plenty of accessories and outfits were available for Michele; she could have a cot, highchair, playpen, toy car, potty, brush and comb – the smaller items were included as extras in the clothing packs. Amongst the outfits were a super fur coat and hat, a summer smock, nightie, rompers, playsuit and a party dress. Michele cost 32/11 (£1.65), while her cot was only a few pennies cheaper at 32/6 (£1.62). Her high chair was 17/6 (87p). Many of her accessories were made from white plastic and decorated with colourful transfers. In 1969 the Consumer Association's *Which?* magazine included Michele in a review of dolls (see Chapter 3) and concluded she was the best buy. The version which they tested was the updated doll with follow-me lenticular eyes. Unfortunately, Michele's body was made from foam rubber which tended to deteriorate, and so today she isn't particularly easy to find – no doubt, as the doll crumbled, she was placed in the bin.

Roddy

Also known as D.G. Todd (see Chapter 2), just as in the 1950s, this company produced many beautiful, quality dolls. Although they embraced the new vinyl plastic, it is interesting to note that many of the Roddy hard plastic dolls were not immediately discontinued and continued being made until well into the 1960s. It is worth noting too that often the vinyl Roddy dolls don't bear the company name, however they are usually marked

**Solemn-faced
Roddy girl**

'Made in England' which is arranged in a small circle on their backs. Many of the Roddy vinyl dolls have very delicate colouring, and one which was particularly popular was a pretty, solemn-faced girl who originally appeared in hard plastic. Some of the early vinyl dolls had Saran hair. Saran

Roddy girl doll

was a man-made fibre which was rather coarse to touch but which held its style excellently.

As with many other companies at the time, Roddy sometimes made dolls with the new vinyl heads but with hard plastic bodies. This was partly due to the cost of changing all the machinery in one go, but also because dolls made completely using the early vinyl technique could become very heavy, especially for smaller children to carry around. Once blow moulding took over from rotational casting, dolls became lighter. The D.G. Todd company used an excellent, firm quality vinyl, and this is no doubt why so many Roddy dolls survive. The major weakness with some Roddy dolls is that the eye construction technique involved two tiny lugs, and the eyes had a tendency to slip after a while. Although the vinyl Roddys are sometimes found with their eyes slightly pushed in, they can normally be re-positioned by the skilful use of a pair of tweezers and maybe a dab of glue on the lugs which hold the eyes in place. In the late sixties the company changed hands, passing to Alex and James Smith, who registered the trademark 'Bluebell'. Bluebell continued to produce dolls, such as the innovative early 1970s' Miss Happy Heart.

Roddy made several of their dolls in large sizes, and these often found their way into the windows of babywear shops, as they made excellent manikins, modelling the garments. Many of their dolls had delightful, rounded faces with full cheeks and rosy colouring. Their hair was short and curly and they had slightly open mouths which gave them charming expressions. Amongst the babies was a moulded-hair cutie with a delightful shy smile, and her face is regarded by collectors as one of the classic Roddy faces. One of the prettiest of the 1960s' Roddy/Bluebell dolls was Choosy

'Anyone for tennis?!' Girl doll by Roddy

**Large toddler
doll by Roddy**

Susie. Roddy frequently sold undressed versions of their dolls to other companies, such as the Gwyneth Doll Company, who clothed them in traditional Welsh costumes. As Bluebell still utilised Roddy moulds, sometimes dolls were marked 'Roddy' but the packaging said 'Bluebell'. Consequently, Roddy collectors have a dilemma – are these dolls classed Bluebell or Roddy?!

Shelley Cuff recalls, 'As a child of the sixties I have quite a few dolly memories. One of my first dolls was a small vinyl Roddy baby with moulded hair. I actually called it Roddy but wasn't over keen on it. My next memory was of a vinyl doll with short pink rooted hair; I was given her around 1964 but again wasn't keen. In fact the doll was unceremoniously dumped out of the new Silver Cross pram and my dearly loved teddy, Yogi, was given pride of place. He rode around in the pram often. I think what I really wanted was a doll with long hair and I kept getting short curly-haired ones. Even now I am not keen on short-haired dolls and am attracted to long-haired ones. Sometime in the late sixties I was given a beautiful slender doll with a mass of white blonde hair by my aunt and uncle. There were four cousins in the family and they brought one back for each of us from their holidays. I was lucky enough to have first pick. I picked that particular doll because she reminded me of Aqua Marina from Stingray.'

Choosy Susie was registered by D.G. Todd in 1967, and sold under the Bluebell name. Her distinctive, pretty face featured an open mouth with two fairly large teeth – necessary to hide a magnet. She had sleep-eyes and short hair cut into a baby bob. Sturdy, well-moulded with expressive hands, she was a bent-limbed toddler, 20 inches tall, though slightly let down by her body which was of a softer, thinner vinyl. When her head was gently touched, it wobbled. Susie's hidden magnet mechanism allowed her to choose her food. She was sold with two 'spoons', one with an enjoyable treat, the other not such a pleasant food. If she was offered the treat, she would turn her head towards the spoon – but she quickly swivelled away from the yukky food! Prettily dressed in a blue or lemon angel top with a white pinafore over the top, decorated with two large daisies, Susie was advertised as 'The baby doll with a mind of her own.' Collector Sharon White who has been trying to replace her favourite

Choosy Susie by Roddy

childhood dolls, says, 'I haven't yet been able to replace my Choosy Susie. You could offer her milk and she'd accept that happily but if you offered her a spoon with "greens" on it, she'd turn her head away.'

Rosebud

As we saw in Chapter 2, Rosebud was the name which Nene Plastics used for their range of attractive dolls. In 1960 the company purchased a new factory at Wellingborough, Northants, for doll production. From here poured millions of dolls. Printed on their boxes was the slogan 'Rosebud, Britain's Most Loveable Dolls'.

An early 1960s' catalogue urges 'Pick a Rosebud', and contains a selection of beautiful dolls, though sadly they are unnamed. Amongst them is a sleeping baby with short nylon hair who was available in three sizes – 11 inches, 14 inches and 19 inches, and who was sold in a dainty rosebud-print nylon lace-trimmed dress and matching bonnet. The smallest size cost 33/- (£1.65) and the largest was 68/3 (£3.42). It also offers four different sizes of a baby doll with moulded hair and a very sweet face, ranging from 11 inches to 25 inches high, and advertises a bath set containing an 11-inch doll with rooted hair and a bath, potty, talc, soap, brush, comb, towel and several other bath necessities. This set cost 37/9 (£1.89).

A 'life-size' baby doll, sold in size 25 inches (six months) or 30 inches (one year), dressed in a pretty flower-sprigged organza dress and lavishly frilled bonnet, cost £6/11/6 (£6.58) for the smaller

Rosebud catalogue

Rosebud babies

size and £8/1/6 (£8.08) for the larger. This sturdy doll had a sweetly smiling face with a slightly open mouth and sleeping eyes. Even dearer was a 'life-size walking two-year-old', 31 inches high, with short hair, shy smile, dimpled knees, wearing a pretty puffed-sleeve cotton dress with an apron, and who sold for £9/2/0 (£9.10).

Amongst the girl dolls was one with either short pink or blue hair available in three sizes, a 'dusky' doll in a 'gay cotton two-piece' and a large girl, 26 inches tall, in a colourful cotton dress with rooted superfine nylon hair. In addition there was a series of girls with blonde or brunette hair in various styles, neatly dressed in cotton frocks – younger girls still tended to wear dresses rather than trousers then – in assorted sizes, many using the moulds from the earlier hard plastic days.

In 1962 an advert in *Woman's Own* appeared for Mandy, a '15-inch washable doll complete with clothes'. Selling for 13/6d (67p), the blurb reads, 'Introducing Mandy – she's waiting to make a lucky little girl jump for joy on Christmas morning. She comes complete with this candy striped dress, shoes and socks. Her lovely blonde hair can be shampooed, set and combed without losing its curl. She can sit and stand and her twinkling blue eyes open and shut as well. Made specially by the manufacturers of Rosebud dolls, she just can't break and she doesn't mind how often she's washed. Her face and arms are made of vinyl which feels as

Rosebud 'Baby Angel'

soft as skin. What a present for so little!'

1962 also saw the introduction of 'Wonder Baby' which was a similar principle to the American (Ideal) Thumbelina doll (see Chapter 10). The Rosebud Wonder Baby, which retailed at £4.19.6 (£4.98) was operated by an 'unbreakable' clockwork unit. The doll wriggled, moved her head, sucked her thumb and held her toes. She was 20 inches long, and dressed in a blue and

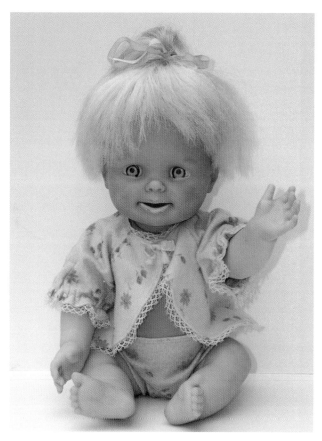

Cheerful Tearful by Rosebud could smile . . .

white knitted romper-suit. This chubby-faced baby doll was advertised on television, as well as in the press as part of a major campaign (along with Chatty Cathy).

In the mid-sixties, the Rosebud company began planning large export drives to various countries including America, Canada, Japan and South Africa, but surprisingly, a spokesman said that in all countries white dolls sold the best. Though they had tried a black doll, it hadn't proved successful and had consequently been dropped from the range. Slightly later they introduced various feeding and wetting baby dolls, such as 'Baby Angel', a 16-inch high doll with thick blonde hair. Originally dressed in a lemon rose-print outfit, she had blue sleep-eyes and an open mouth with a small hole to take the teat of the bottle. Rosebud also produced Chatty Cathy, using Mattel speech mechanisms (see Chapter 9), and Cheerful Tearful.

. . . and pout

Cheerful Tearful, who was marked Mattel 1965 but sold by Rosebud, was one of the top-selling dolls of the time. Her face was slightly rubbery, with an armature beneath, and the raising of her arm caused her to change expression from a smile to a pout, a similar idea to Pedigree's Baby Sparkle and Palitoy's Pouting Pretti. This clever Cheerful Tearful was 12 inches high, and was sold in a pink, rose-printed brushed cotton top and pants with matching bootees. She had blue transfer eyes and short blonde hair with a top knot. Her box proclaimed: 'Raise my left arm all the way up to make me smile. Lower my left arm all the way down to make me pout and cry "waaa"! Feed me water from my own bottle. I cry real tears and wet too! No batteries needed.'

In 1967, the company was acquired by Mattel – by then, their annual sales were in excess of £1,000,000, and the American influence was already being felt. They began to use the name Rosebud-Mattel, before discarding the 'Rosebud' in the early 1970s. Mattel had worked closely with Rosebud for some time before the merger, and had provided the technology for the various speech mechanisms used in the Rosebud and the Chatty Cathy series of dolls. However, a few years later the Wellingborough factory became Rotary Plastics, and they decided to apply for permission to use the Rosebud name, because Mattel was no longer using it. As permission was refused, they took the name of Blossom Toys, and started producing a large range of dolls.

Various

Many other dolls were around in Britain in the 1960s, some one-offs by obscure makers, some imported from Hong Kong and other countries, while a huge amount were completely unmarked and so today's collector has to make a guess at where they might have originated. Major companies often omitted their brand name when they were selling their dolls under the label of a store; for instance, Pedigree and Chiltern sometimes sold through Woolworths, which is why a familiar-faced doll might bear no markings.

It's also difficult to date some of these unmarked or unrecorded dolls, unless you have some kind of provenance such as a receipt or advertise-

Kelly 'The Sunshine Girl', offered by Kellogg's

ment. Dolls were frequently offered through magazines and grocery products, either for cash or for token collect. An example is Kelly, 'The Sunshine Girl', who was a Kellogg's token collect. Isle of Wight collector Lesley Glover says, 'I believe she was offered by Kellogg's in 1966 and came with her own knitting pattern which I tracked down for my doll. Kelly is 12 inches high and has blow-moulded arms and legs, with the arms being strung. The head is soft vinyl with sparkling blue glassine eyes and thick eyelashes. She is marked "Made in England" in a line on her neck

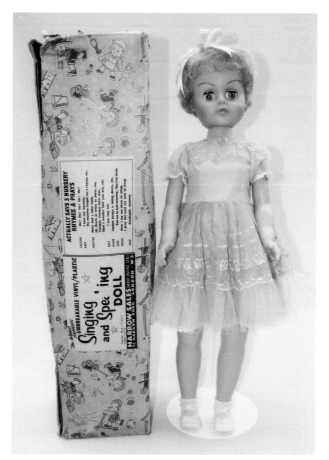

**Singing doll by
Mark Payne**

and "Made in England" in capitals on her back. Kelly is wearing all her original clothes including lacy nylon type pants and socks. Her shoes are marked "Made in England" on the heels. I also have some clothes from the pattern book which came with her.'

Popular during the 1960s and 70s were large, lightweight plastic dolls sold by the Mark Payne Company in London under the name 'Singing Doll Company' (see *British Dolls of the 1950s*). These dolls were made in Hong Kong and stood 24 inches high. They seemed rather top-heavy and were inclined to fall as the body, containing the mechanism, was quite weighty for the legs to support. The dolls came with either a built-in mechanism operated by turning a handle, or, later, were battery-operated with interchangeable records, and could sing many nursery rhymes, as well as having a repertoire of phrases. They were advertised in many newspapers and magazines of the time, impressively listing all the songs the dolls could perform. I remember poring over these adverts with longing, though in the 1960s I was considered too old for dolls. I recently acquired one, because as you get older, surprisingly, doll collecting is considered perfectly acceptable!

Rosebud mint in box girl

Chapter 7

Lesser Companies

Lots of smaller or lesser-known companies also produced dolls during the 1960s, and many of them were of excellent quality. Though some fell by the wayside, others have become collector's items and are much sought after today. Girls tended to play with larger dolls, unlike today when the small fashion doll seems more in vogue, and so dolls' prams, cots and cradles were popular. Also, people still enjoyed knitting and sewing (see my book *British Dolls of the 1950s*) and patterns and sewing kits were widely available. Several companies sold ranges of dolls' clothes, however, for those without the time, or inclination, to sew.

Airfix

This company, more renowned for its plastic model kits than its dolls, did venture into the doll world occasionally. Originally set up in the late 1930s as a manufacturer of rubber toys, it later began making combs, soon being Britain's largest maker of the product. They soared to fame in the 1950s with their model kits, and in the early 60s took over several companies, including Semco Ltd., a company who made small baby dolls for Woolworths.

Airfix retained the Semco name and issued some extra large (27-inch) dolls under licence from Disney; these are marked as copyright Disney, whilst a further range just says, 'Semco Ltd. 1964'. Roberta Snape, a collector and doll fair organiser, owns a boxed 19 inches high Mary Poppins doll dating from the 1960s. The doll is marked Semco, and the box, too, is labelled. Says Roberta, 'The boxed one says "An Airfix doll manufactured by the Semco division, Made in England. MCMLXIV Walt Disney Productions". Also, I have a newspaper advert for my boxed doll, dated December 16 1965. Her original price was 69/11d. She is a lovely doll.'

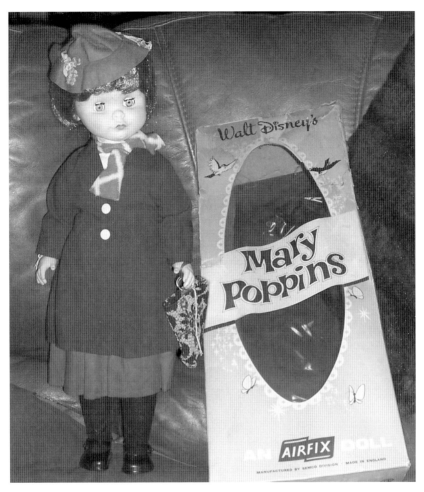

Airfix/Semco Mary Poppins

Amanda Jane

In Chapter 4 I explained how a dreadful fire meant that the Amanda Jane company had to start again from scratch, and they introduced an 8-inch girl doll called Amanda Jane. Although we tend to associate the Amanda Jane company with a range of small, 8-inch high girl dolls, including Jinx, a small hard plastic doll, the company also sold other examples, as well as a range of clothes and accessories. My previous book, *British Dolls of the 1950s*, tells how the company was formed.

Amanda by Clodrey for Amanda Jane

Before the fire the Amanda Jane company was marketing a range of dolls produced by various companies, including the Clodrey company of France, Gaeltarra Eireann – a company in Southern Ireland who were manufacturers of Crolly dolls – and G. & S. of Watford, Hertfordshire. They had also introduced a small, 8-inch girl called Jinny. Jinny was similar to Jinx but had rooted hair with a body similar to that of the later vinyl Amanda Jane. The Jinny heads were made by Palitoy, but the records seem non-existent. It is likely that Jinny dolls are those marked 'Amanda Jane' but with a waxy appearance and pale, shiny eyelids. When compared to a sleep-eyed Amanda Jane, the latter seems to have a squarer jaw. I have occasionally seen these heads on hard plastic Jinx bodies, and believe they are rare transitional dolls, before the Jinny head was placed on an Amanda Jane body. They too were discontinued after the fire.

The large Amanda doll was produced by Clodrey. She was 13 inches tall and made from blown polythene with rooted hair. According to the

Amanda Jane company, she featured 'patent magic eyes that follow you everywhere'. Her back was marked 'Made in France, Polyflex' together with an odd symbol. At first glance it resembled a fleur de lis, but on closer inspection it was revealed as a balance with a stork and a phoenix.

This doll was featured in an early Amanda Jane leaflet which used her as its model in most of the pictures. The accompanying text read, 'The doll shown in all the pictures (except those illustrating Jinx) is: 5012 Amanda 12 in. (30 cm.) Retail Price 29/6d. With superior Saran hair. Made of resilient polythene, the very latest thing in doll manufacture, she weighs only 6 ounces, has rooted hair which is washable and combable and sleeping eyes and she is fully jointed. No unpleasant odour such as that characteristic of vinyl.' Incidentally, it is interesting to note that Amanda's size is given as 12 inches, yet another publicity leaflet says Amanda is 13 inches high. Having measured the doll, I can tell you that the correct height is 13 inches!

An article in *The Observer*, December 1960, which referred to the Amanda doll as the 'Amanda Jane' doll, stated that she took a size 12 (12-inch) outfit. The price of the riding outfit was 13/6d (68p), while 'Duet', a lace-trimmed dress 'with its own pants', cost 12/6d (63p). This article stated that the company 'markets only two dolls. Amanda Jane herself – resilient polythene with rooted washable and combable hair, sleeping eyes and fully-jointed at 29/11d. And Jinx, an eight-inch charmer in hard plastic with

Jane by Gaeltarra Eireann for Amanda Jane

brushable, combable hair at 3/11d'. Incidentally, these prices shed a fascinating light on the collecting world – today, the Amanda Jane doll (which
was over six times the price of the Jinx – £1.49 as opposed to 19p for the
latter) – now only sells for around £12, as opposed to £50 for Jinx!

However, it wasn't long before they introduced Jane, made by Gaeltarra
Eireann, who was 12 inches tall and Bubbles, from G. & S., a 14-inch baby
girl. Both Jane and Bubbles were all-vinyl dolls with rooted hair. Jane bore
the words 'Crolly Doll Made in the Republic of Ireland' on her back,
while baby Bubbles was marked 'Amanda Jane Made in England'. Rather
disrespectfully, the girls – Amanda, Jane, Jinx and Jinny – were referred to
as 'tubby girls' in the advertising leaflets! In 1963, Amanda retailed at
19/11d (99p), Jane 15/6d (78p), Bubbles 19/11d (99p), Jinx at 3/11d (19p)
and Jinny 7/11d (39p). Obviously, the company didn't believe in rounding
up the prices.

A very rare set of Amanda Jane dolls were called Nursery Rhyme dolls.
These were all vinyl and stood 13 inches high with rooted hair. They date

**Chain store
brand dolls
ready for
dressing**

from 1965, but were only sold for around three months as they were destroyed in the fire. The dolls used new moulds and their clothes were based on illustrations from a children's book published by W.M. Collins. There were six different costume designs. The Amanda Jane company also have a brief and intriguing mention in their records for 1965: '300D revolutionary new departure in doll design commissioned by Amanda Jane from designer Fredun Shapur. (Moulds eventually sold to Friedland Doggatt, makers of Sasha).' Whether they were ever produced by this company – owners of Frido – is unclear.

Chain Store Brands

It's interesting to seek out dolls which were sold under the brand names of various stores and shops. These dolls were often manufactured by major companies, but were dressed and packaged to the store's requirements. Usually, the dolls would have the regular maker's name (i.e. Pedigree) removed from the doll, which means that today, unless you find the doll in its original packaging, or with its swing tags or labels, it is very difficult to identify. Retailers such as Tesco (Delaware), Woolworths (Winfield), Marks and Spencer (St Michael), Littlewoods (Keynote) or British Home Stores (Prova) all sold dolls, as did many others. Woolworths were so prolific with their Winfield Little Beauty range that they are mentioned later in this chapter, as well as in Chapter 2.

Ranella, Lewis's doll

Another interesting one to look out for is Ranella, a brand name used by Lewis's, a Northern chain of stores. They issued a pretty 13-inch high girl doll in the late 1960s, which sold for 19/11d (99p). Her name was Miss Ranella, and a huge range of fashionable outfits was available to buy separately, including day dresses, party wear, leisure wear, coats and various accessories. A note on her box read: 'It's lovely to think that you are going to be my new mummy. I'm sure you will want to know about the pretty clothes you can get for me at Lewis's, all specially made in my size. I just love dressing up, don't you?' She goes on to say, 'Did I tell you that you can only get my Ranella clothes and things from Lewis's? The nice part about it is that Lewis's keep adding items so I'll be right in fashion.' An early example of pester power?

Maria by Frido

Frido

Frido, who also used the name Frida for their doll range, were based in Reddish, Stockport and were part of the Friedland group, famed for their door chimes. In the early sixties, Frido was known as a general toy and doll manufacturer, later becoming famed for their range of Sasha dolls (see Chapter 4).

The company also produced a range of vinyl dolls, amongst them some very attractive and unusual designs. Interestingly, some of the Frido dolls are identical to Chiltern, so presumably the companies shared or traded moulds. A browse through the catalogues reveals some extremely lovely dolls, the majority being 15 or 18 inches tall. There are lots of black dolls included in the

range, all beautifully dressed.
Amongst them are a nursing sister, a
nanny with a baby, a Parisienne
maid, a flower-seller and a
'mammie' – it is quite unusual to
find such a large range of black dolls.
Also shown is a particularly
delightful black girl, Mitzi, wearing
a white organdie party dress, and
holding a bouquet of flowers.

Other 1960s' Frida dolls from
Frido include a short-haired blonde
nurse doll wearing a pale blue
uniform and holding a 'detachable

Metal tag attached to Frido dolls

baby', a bride in a full-skirted wedding dress with a long net veil, a group
of dolls in pretty cotton frocks with their hair scooped up into a fashionable sixties topknot tied with a bow, Carol the artist dressed in a blue
smock, red tights and floppy hat holding a brush and palette, and black-
haired Maria who wears 'a delightfully gay dress' in red cotton with a blue
and white striped panel on the bodice. Frido also made several delightful
soft-bodied babies, some 12-inch tall girls with distinctive out-turned
hands and round mouths, and a cheeky-looking freckled-faced baby called
Ivy, which has been labelled 'Grows on you'! The dolls were sold in
colourful boxes decorated with pictures of children with balloons, pets and
flowers, and each doll bore a large metal tag on her wrist proclaiming it
was a 'Seal of Guarantee'.

Gaeltarra Eireann

This company, situated in Southern Ireland, began in 1939 in a factory
at Crolly, County Donegal. It was set up as part of a new industry to
manufacture toys and various utility products by the Gaeltacht Services
Division of the Department of Lands, and there were two other factories
involved, one in Mayo (Elly Bay Co.) for soft toys and bears, and the
other at Spiddal, County Galway, for lead toys. Apparently, the industry

Crolly girl doll

was administered by the Civil Service and was subsidised by the state, with an emphasis on job creation. Initially, the dolls were composition with soft bodies, dressed using local fabrics. There was a considerable demand for toys during the war, and afterwards the company began experimenting with vinyl, soon producing attractive and robust dolls of various sizes. It's said that long queues formed outside stores at Christmas, and customers were limited to one or two dolls each – they were popular because of their excellent quality. The Crolly tradename was registered in 1956 by Gaeltarra Eireann.

In 1969, the Elly Bay factory closed, and the soft toy manufacturing was transferred to the Crolly factory, but the quality declined and most of the teddies were unjointed and used synthetics rather than mohair. The company continued manufacturing both dolls and teddies until 1970, but then ceased, primarily because of cheap imports. Today, there is still a factory known as Crolly, but it is not related to the original Crolly factory, although it still makes high quality dolls for both children and collectors.

Kader

It is difficult to find out much about the early days of the Hong Kong-based factory, Kader, but they produced a large range of inexpensive dolls made from a distinctive shiny, brittle plastic, as mentioned in my book *British Dolls of the 1950s*. Many similar dolls bearing such names as Evergreen, Camay and Agrespoly were also around, possibly made at the same factory, as they seem identical. The dolls, which originated in the 1950s, continued to be sold throughout the 60s and well into the 1970s, not only from local corner shops but major stores, too. Because of their styling, they can appear older than they actually are – few other dolls from this period feature the moving tongues and twisting wrists of the Kader types.

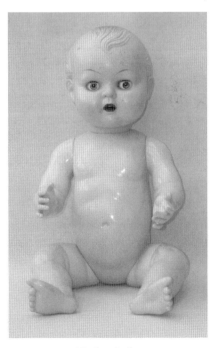

The plastic, though brittle, is, in many cases, of an excellent quality; the later dolls feature a softer vinyl/plastic. Kader dolls are marked 'OK' Kader on their backs, together with a globe, while Camay, Evergreen and the others are also labelled accordingly. Most commonly found are bald-headed babies in a variety of sizes, from 3 inches upwards. Very large teen

Kader baby

dolls were also made, and boy dolls with hair moulded in a side parting. Some of the girls with the moulded, fringed hair resemble 1930s' dolls and are particularly charming.

Little Beauty

Many stores sold dolls under their own brand names at this time, but the Little Beauty range which was sold by Woolworths from 1964, under their brand name Winfield, seems to crop up more regularly than most (see Chapter 2).

The dolls, which were of various heights, were made from a high quality soft-touch vinyl which had a slight vanilla scent. They had long lustrous rooted hair with a glossy sheen, and were jointed at neck, shoulders and hips. They were completely washable and were sold in pretty boxes featuring a ribbon design. The range included girl dolls, babies and teens,

Winfield 'Little Beauty' girl

**Winfield doll
who featured as
Hamble in
*Playschool***

and amongst them was a doll destined to be a star – in fact, one who has now risen to the heights of a 'cult doll'!

This doll, later known as Hamble, was one of the Little Beauty dolls, and was chosen to be one of the regulars of the BBC programme for small children, *Playschool*, which began broadcasting in 1964. Hamble was 19 inches high, and was sold with blonde or brunette short curly hair (the one used on television was brunette). She was soft-bodied – the body was made of pink cloth – with vinyl limbs, and featured a rather screwed-up face, almost a caricature, with a slightly open mouth revealing a tongue. Her eyes were fixed glassine, and she had hair lashes and painted brows. The hair of the brunette had a tendency to develop a green tinge over the years, presumably a reaction to sunshine.

The Little Beauty (surely a misnomer in this case!) Hamble doll featured in *Playschool* alongside Humpty (a round soft toy), Jemima (a long-legged rag doll) Big Ted and Little Ted (teddy bears), but, according to accounts, was disliked by the presenters because she was ugly and didn't sit up properly. In the 1970s, she was replaced by an all-plastic version. Today, the Little Beauty doll – which isn't actually labelled as Hamble but is instantly recognisable – sells for quite a high price, as it has now taken its place alongside other items of 1960s' media memorabilia.

Prams and Paraphernalia

Coach-built prams with shiny sides, bouncy springs and gaberdine hoods with storm-covers were made in their thousands, although soft-bodied types were available too. Pushchairs, cots, highchairs, baby walkers, playpens, as well as smaller accessories such as feeding bottles, rattles and dummies were sold – as they still are today – but in the sixties, there was a much wider choice, because the big takeovers were yet to come. There were plenty of independent manufacturers and toy shops, so children and their parents weren't compelled to buy from just one or two major ranges.

Companies such as Tri-ang took full-page adverts in magazines to announce their new lines. In the early 1960s, Tri-ang offered a top-of-the-range Classic pram: 'A neat, elegant model of the Pedigree baby carriage. 27 ins body, 29 ins handle height. £13.19.6d' (£13.98), or 'Consort –

Tri-ang pram

Leeway pram

Delightful dolls pram with lift-off body. Handle height 29 ins. £8.7.6d' (£8.38). Particularly cute was the Robin de Luxe: 'A charming pram with 16ins body. The handle height is 20 ins. £1.19.11d' (£1.99). This was a small round-bodied type with a floral hood and apron, suitable for the smaller child to push. They made carrycots which fitted into a frame, too, such as the 'No.2 De luxe Stroller and Crib – 24 ins, lined crib in fabric – fits snugly into the folding tubular stroller. £5.17.6d' (£5.88). Pushchairs included the 'Dolls Pedypak – Just Right for Shopping – folding pushchair with bag attached. Handle height 29ins. £2.9.11d' (£2.49).

Tri-ang also produced many other toys which appealed to doll-loving children. There was a smart, blue convertible doll's highchair. The chair could be lifted off to form a low chair and stool. A blue bath, 18 inches long, which fitted neatly into its own metal stand, cost £1.5.6 (£1.28p), while an ironing board, at 15/6d (78p) was perfect for ironing all those dolly dresses after they had been laundered.

One of the most renowned of the pram companies was Silver Cross, and amongst their 1968 range of superb prams – or doll carriages as they called them – was the Oberon, which featured 'Chromium plated wheels and levers. Cee sprung chassis. Chromium décor on body. Available in the exclusive colour combination of rolls grey coachwork, royal blue hood and apron and navy interior. Price £16.12.6d' (£16.63p). Top of the range was the Super Twin, which retailed at £17.17.6d (£17.88p).

Wearing Apparel

Companies such as Faerie Glen, Amanda Jane, Rosebud and Tri-ang ('Mam'selle'), sold ranges of dolls' clothes to fit all kinds, from the smallest

Dolls' clothes were sold to fit all sizes

to the largest, and so children could readily kit out their dolls in the latest styles. Chain stores, too, sold their own outfits made specially for them by manufacturers in Britain or abroad; children couldn't afford to buy dolls regularly, but a pretty dress or trendy set of separates might well persuade them to part with their pocket money.

So the dolls' clothes were around in abundance, hanging from counter displays in toy shops, filling baskets and boxes. There were packs of shoes, hats, undies, even jewellery, and in those days, when shopkeepers had more patience, they would humour a small child who took her favourite dolly to the shop in search of a new dress or pair of shoes. It's intriguing to look out for these 1960s' clothes today, because they tell the story of the decade's fashions, beginning with stylish, tailored shirt-waisted dresses, formal ball-gowns or flouncy skirts with net petticoats, and ending with op art shifts, ultra-short mini-dresses – and, of course, flowers, especially round-petalled daisies, scattered over everything!

Many of the outfits are labelled with the manufacturer, but others, though obviously factory-made, bear no clues. Some were intended to complement certain dolls, such as the Tiny Tears' outfits by Palitoy (see Chapter 5) and the Sindy clothes made by Pedigree, but many others were general ranges, advertised as fitting any favourite doll, and consequently it's often possible to find the same garment in several sizes.

The Amanda Jane company (see Chapter 3), made a full range of clothing in the very early sixties, not only to fit its own range of Jinx, Amanda and Jane dolls, but also to cater for many other types of dolls, from 8-inch to 22-inch high, and for shapes from 'tubby' to 'model'! The company also sold 'Young Dressmaker' kits for girls who wanted to sew their own dolls' clothes. A catalogue issued in 1960 featured an impressive range of garments; anything a child could possibly need for her doll is there. Colourful, full-skirted cotton dresses bore such names as 'Bon Appetit', 'Lido', 'Checkmate', 'Calypso', 'Aperitif' and 'Dixieland', and sold between 1/11d (19p) and 9/11d (49p). 'Fantasy' was a cute three-piece sunsuit in printed cotton complete with a coolie hat, 'Riviera' was a cotton print flared dress with a straw hat, and 'St. Ada's Boniface' was a smart school blouse and gymslip. The blazer, hat and satchel were all available separately.

Teen dolls could wear 'Swiss Miss' ('Flowered organdie, puff sleeves,

Faerie Glen outfit

trimmed with lace and featuring a velvet bodice'), 'Square Rig' ('Felt duffle with tartan collar and drainpipe trews') and 'Petruska' ('Fur coat and cossack hat lined with taffeta in bright colours, pompom on hat'). Accessories for dolls included wellington boots, Cinderella shoes, carpet slippers, hats, wardrobe, desk and chair, blackboards in three sizes, sunglasses, jewellery, baskets and even tiny writing sets. However, after the fire at the factory (see Chapter 3), in which most of the patterns and stock perished, Amanda Jane decided to concentrate on their new, 8-inch Amanda Jane vinyl girl and her outfits, drastically reducing their huge range of garments for other dolls. These later, small Amanda Jane outfits were a super reflection of the sixties, with 'flower power' themed trouser suits and dresses, and vividly coloured geometric design garments.

In 1960, Faerie Glen Wear proclaimed, 'Faerie Glen Wear makes it possible to collect, at very reasonable prices, nearly everything that your doll needs to be well dressed for all occasions. All outfits are branded with the Faerie Glen label and have buttons and loops for ease of dressing and adjustment for size if required.' They went on to explain that their garments could be obtained in five sizes (beginning with 9 inches, up to 22 inches) plus a new special range for slim teenage dolls, as well as a range for the company's Tonie and Sally, who were two 8-inch hard plastic dolls.

The catalogue depicted the outfits modelled on real dolls, unlike the early Mam'selle and Amanda Jane catalogues which relied on drawings, and many were identified by girls' names, rather than the fanciful names used by other companies. For instance, 'Joan' and 'Brenda' were the names given to two frocks 'in gay cotton' – the price of Joan's dress ranged from 2/- (10p) to 5/6d (28p), Brenda's was 6d (3p) more, while Eileen's 'Multi-spot cotton and rayon frock' was priced from 3/11d (19p) to 7/6d (38p), depending on size.

Rosebud, famed for their dolls, also sold dress sets. Their advert read: 'It's such fun for a child to dress her doll in clothes that have been specially designed for it by Rosebud. And there are Rosebud dress sets for dolls of all sizes. For a treat, take her to the toy shop and let her choose! See them at toy shops and stores today!'

The 'Teenage range' bore an explanation: 'A new kind of doll is now becoming very popular. These are the tall slim bodied teenage doll. As our normal range of clothing is not suitable for these dolls we introduce on the next three pages a special range for them.' The catalogue said that the teen dresses were 'made in three sizes, T–10/12", T–13/16", T–17/20". The "T" indicates Teenage fitting'. Here were a selection of up-to-the-minute styles which included tartan trews, a candy striped full-skirted frock with

Stockings for teen dolls by Faerie Glen

**Faerie Glen
outfit**

matching beach hat, a nylon seersucker dress trimmed at the waist with satin ribbon and a taffeta-lined winter coat.

In this catalogue, teen accessories weren't mentioned, though nylon stockings were promised 'shortly', but there were plenty of extras for the girl dolls; slippers, sandals, socks, wellingtons, hats, wigs, panties and jewellery. A slightly later catalogue lists a school satchel 'containing note-book, tables, rubber, ruler and pencil' at 3/11d (19p), a suitcase at 7/11d (39p), decorated with 'gay travel labels' and a wooden wardrobe with sliding doors, which cost 19/11d (99p).

In 1962 Faerie Glen introduced their own 15-inch teen, Gigi, and sold many fashions for her, both casual and sophisticated, amongst them an extremely elegant fantail black lace over red taffeta evening dress complete with a net stole; a flocked white nylon ball-gown, trimmed with black and golden braid and featuring a black strapless velveteen bodice; and 'Off beat trews and loose box shirt with handy duffle bag'.

Tri-ang (Pedigree) also issued small booklets illustrating their Mam'selle fashion range, which covered all kinds of dolls, from 10-inch to 22-inch girl dolls, and 16- and 20-inch teens. (Later, they included styles for the smaller teens.) The booklets were labelled, 'For Fashion Conscious Dolls' and, as was often the custom in the early sixties, illustrated with black and white line drawings – rather glamourised – of the outfits, the dolls being drawn as real people. Amongst the range are such delights as 'Lambeth Walk', a girl's coat described as, 'Smart town coat in grey/white shepherd's check with white fur collar', 'Tulip Time' ('Floral patterned cotton dirndl dress'), 'Ocean Wave' ('Graceful sea blue satin party frock with dainty lace sleeves and trimmings') and 'Sugar Candy' ('Rayon flowered print [full-skirted frock] on blue background, trimmed with coloured ribbon'). Other outfits included a fairy, nurse, sailor suit, cowgirl, Girl Guide, Brownie, bride and 'jodhpur set', all in various sizes. There was also that item so typical of the time – an all-over elasticated, ruched bathing costume. Accessories included a toilet set comprising soap, toothbrush, toothpaste, sponge and monogrammed towel, a handbag set, brush, comb and mirror, and even a doll's pram for a doll to push.

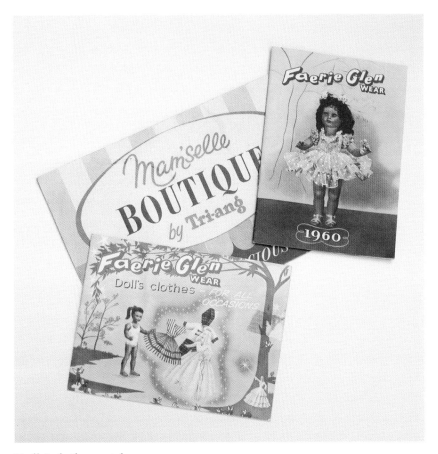

Dolls' clothes catalogues

The large teen dolls were well-catered for, too – the 1961 catalogue described lots of full-skirted dresses in pretty cotton prints, so evocative of the early sixties, with, of course, that vital accessory which every fashionable teen needed at the time; a 'bouffant nylon waist slip, lace trimmed, available in pink or blue', to make those dresses really stick out. Further teen accessories include a selection of 'jewellery' comprising brooches, pearl necklets, earrings and pendants, as well as handbags, hats, and that other 1960s' must-have, a cotton kitchen apron!

A year later, there was a great improvement in the catalogue – the sketches were now in colour, which made the fashions easier to visualise, even though when the actual garments were compared with the pictures, there was still a great deal of artistic licence. Still, now we could see the pink flowers on the embossed cotton dress of 'Carousel' and the bright blue Lurex net over the white pique skirt of 'Starlight', while the teens demonstrated the pretty pink and blue weave of the 'Oklahoma' dress and the orange cotton of the straight dress known as 'Bingo Queen'! This catalogue also included some garments to fit 25-inch baby dolls.

Of course, by 1963, Pedigree had launched the Sindy range of outfits, and gradually, the Sindy-sized dolls had ousted the larger teens. However, in 1965, Mam'selle introduced a range of garments for the new-sized small teens, which were useful budget buys for children who couldn't afford the authentic Sindy clothes.

Sewing and Knitting

The 'make do and mend' ideal of the previous decades still lingered in the 1960s, and most girls could knit, sew and embroider. Many teens made their own dresses, too, and pattern companies prided themselves on producing simple patterns with a minimum of seams, which even those with the most basic sewing skills could make. Although I could knit and embroider nicely, my sewing skills weren't advanced, yet I was able to create a number of dresses for myself in the mid-sixties by using simple patterns. One favourite was a kaftan-shaped knee-length dress which consisted of only two pieces! I made it in several colours, with assorted

Hundreds of patterns were sold for dolls' outfits

trims, and it meant I could be fashionable even though I couldn't afford to buy many ready-made garments.

Patterns for dolls' clothes appeared in many women's magazines, and there was often a doll to send off for, as well. Haberdashery shops, too, were full of dolls' patterns, both knitting and sewing, and today, a look round any doll fair will reveal boxes of home-made dolls' clothes. Although some are amateurish, a surprising amount are expertly sewn, lined and trimmed. It is well worth looking out for 1960s' patterns, because they add a fashion dimension to a doll collection, and it's interesting to note the contrast between the sophisticated, adult styles of early 60s' dolls' clothes, and the later, casual, fun garments of the latter part of the decade.

There were many sew-it-yourself dolls' clothes kits around, too, often containing a plastic doll and a selection of ready-to-sew cut-out garments to fit the doll. There were also packs of colourful knitting wool and child-sized needles, to enable children to knit hats, scarves and jumpers for their dolls. Once the Sindy-size dolls were in fashion, dozens of patterns appeared for them, and many children learned to knit by making these clothes, as they didn't need as many stitches or as many rows as a dress for a larger doll.

Dolls look good in knitted outfits

Chapter 8

Dolls for Grown-ups

Thousands of people begin their doll-collecting hobby by buying a costume doll or two when on holiday, and before long realise they have amassed a dozen or so. Then they start looking out for other kinds of dolls.

As a 12-year-old when the 1960s dawned, I had, regretfully, put my 'playing with dolls' years firmly behind me. Schoolwork took up far too much time, and I also had a puppy which needed plenty of exercise. Yet I was still attracted to dolls; my neighbours had a young girl who would sometimes show me her latest doll – made from soft vinyl, with 'real' rooted combable hair, unlike my dolls which were hard plastic and balding because the mohair wigs were wearing thin. Then, one day a school friend went on holiday to Scotland, and she brought me back a little Scottish doll. A light bulb went on in my head – I would look out for dolls in national dress, and collect those. That wouldn't be babyish, that would be an interesting hobby. Not long afterwards, I visited Wales, and there found a doll typically dressed in checked skirt, red cloak and a black 'inverted flowerpot' hat.

However, there was a limit to the number of countries a young schoolgirl could manage to visit in the early 1960s – most people still holidayed in Britain at the time, even a trip to the continent was a

Author's first Welsh doll bought early 1960s

great event – it seemed as though my great idea would founder before it had hardly begun. Then while shopping in Woolworths, to my joy I found a range of 'national costume dolls' from all over the world. The dolls were cheap and cheerful, but they were affordable from my pocket money, and so an Eskimo, sari-clad Indian or Native American would be added to my collection. A camping trip to France yielded a dainty French-costumed celluloid doll, whilst an uncle gave me a miniature doll from Japan. Apart from a couple of large-eyed kitsch dolls and an inflatable Hug-a-Bug (see relevant section), costume dolls were to be the dolls I accumulated in the 1960s. No-one I knew collected large dolls in those days; the only ones considered in any way valuable were made from wax or bisque china, and were in museums.

Costume Dolls

By the mid-sixties, the most commonly-seen costume dolls in the shops included hard plastic dolls sold by the Rexard company, the Woolworths' dolls mentioned above, and quantities of soldiers, sailors and 'Beefeaters' made in Hong Kong which filled the tourist shops around Trafalgar Square and Oxford Street. Rogark Scottish and Welsh dolls, a series of dolls in costumes of the world by Linda dolls and a similar range imported by Codeg could be found, too – costume doll-collecting was extremely popular at the time (see Chapter 2).

More 'upmarket' were dolls by Peggy Nisbet, Shallowpool and those produced by established companies including Roddy and Pedigree, either ready-dressed, or often, sold undressed to tourist centres in Scotland and Wales for them to dress locally. Concerns such as the Gwyneth Doll Company, based in Swansea, bought these dolls, dressing them in traditional Welsh costumes.

Chiltern

The small hard plastic dolls sold through this company during the 1950s were still around in the early 1960s. Standing 7 inches high, with sleep-

Chiltern 'Young' series of costume dolls

eyes, they were jointed at both shoulders and hips. They had glued-on wigs, and appeared in a wide range of costumes. In 1967 a range of 'National Character Dolls' were advertised at 17/9 (88p) each. Amongst the colourful, well-detailed costumes were Young France, Young Japan, Young Holland, Young Poland and Young Switzerland. They also made Bunny Girls, based on the girls from the American nightclubs. According to a catalogue of the time these dolls sold at 8/9 (43p) each, and were dressed in swimsuits. Each also wore 'White plastic cuffs and collar, fluffy bustle and plastic bunny ears'.

Linda

The series of Linda dolls was made in Hong Kong. My book, *British Dolls of the 1950s*, describes the girl dolls produced, using a distinctive

Costume doll by Linda

waxy-looking plastic. The company also made teen dolls of various types and sizes, and dressed many of them in regional and traditional costumes. As well as dolls from other lands, there were British traditional themes, such as a Pearly King and Queen. The dolls were 7½ inches high, and jointed at neck, shoulders and hips. Their backs were marked 'Made in Hong Kong'. They had sleep-eyes (with brown painted lashes above), glued-on wigs and were made from the same waxy plastic. The dolls bore hang tags which read, 'A Linda Durable Plastic Doll Made in Hong Kong' while on the reverse, 'Always ask for Linda. Jointed dolls, Baby dolls, Teenage dolls. Beautifully dressed. Fashionable styles. Wonderful value.' Unlike so many other costume dolls, the majority of the Linda dolls could be played with and undressed, as the clothes featured press studs. Beneath their colourful national costumes, the dolls often wore lace-trimmed nylon panties and plastic bras. It was possible to buy separate outfits for Linda teens, and these are quite easy to identify as most bear a 'Linda' fabric label.

Pedigree

Pedigree had introduced a large range of hard plastic costume dolls in the 1950s, and these continued through to the 1960s. They were small, 7-inch high dolls with rounded faces and, often, distinctive 'starfish' hands with splayed fingers. In the 1960s they brought out a series of Cavalcade dolls, 6 inches tall, dressed as rather unusual characters, such as a judge in his robes and wig, a knight of the garter with insignia and sword, and a bishop with his mitre and crozier. These dolls are not particularly easy to find today, but are worth looking for as they will add variety to the more usual policemen, soldiers or yeomen of the guard normally seen in a collection. At the time, they sold for 19/11d (99p), about twice as much as the standard costume range.

Peggy Nisbet

Peggy Nisbet formed her company in the 1950s, after a doll which she had designed to commemorate the Queen's coronation in 1953 proved popular (see my book *British Dolls of the 1950s* for more details). Her dolls measured between 6 to 8 inches tall – the size varied depending on the range – with

Cavalcade Judge costume doll by Pedigree

hand-painted features. The costumes were researched with painstaking detail, and this was translated into fabric and carefully sewn by a band of talented dressmakers.

There were hundreds of different types of dolls, and they are widely collected today. Categories included British Traditional, National, Historical, Portrait, Shakespeare and 'Happy Dolls'. Happy Dolls were a slightly cheaper, though no less attractive, range. The company was active for around thirty years, and also produced porcelain dolls, limited editions, large vinyl dolls, cloth dolls and teddy bears, which poured forth from the factories and workshops in Weston-super-Mare and Scotland.

After much experimentation, the Peggy Nisbet costume dolls were

**Peggy Nisbet
Hengist, King
of the Angles**

created from an extremely hard vinyl, which is exceptionally durable.
Although the dolls resembled composition, they were constructed from
modern materials. Along the way there were many problems to be sorted,

**Peggy Nisbet
traditional
Eighteenth-
Century English
lady**

such as ensuring Henry VIII's tummy wouldn't collapse, and solving the difficulty of casting his classic 'feet apart' stance. In this case, the feet had to be moulded separately, before attaching them with pins and glue to his legs at the correct angle. Eventually, the dolls evolved into the familiar figures we know today, made from high-impact polystyrene and virtually unbreakable. Unlike the majority of plastic dolls, which at the time were cast in two parts – front and back – and glued together to form a hollow shell, the Nisbet dolls were solid. This was necessary because the brocades and velvets would not hang correctly on a lightweight doll.

There were so many different types of Peggy Nisbet dolls that most people concentrated on collecting certain kinds, or themes. Particularly popular was the Happy Dolls range, previously mentioned. As the clothing on these was not quite so elaborate as that made for the dearer series, it was an ideal way of introducing new outworkers into the techniques required for dressing the dolls. In her autobiography, (see Further Reading), Peggy states, 'New outworkers started with the Happy Dolls, and as they became more expert, they were put on to the more detailed and intricate seven inch dolls.'

Many of the Happy Dolls featured an unusual moulding, with their left leg outstretched and pointing to the side. This was perfect for ballerinas or dancers, but looked a little strange on some of the others in the range.

**Peggy Nisbet
National
Costume
Arabia**

Included in the Happy Dolls were Wendy the schoolgirl, Violet the flower-seller, Emily the Victorian girl, Minnie the parlour maid, Patsy the chorus girl, Bobby the policeman and Sonja the skater. Sonja had skates made by a series of metal punches carefully attached to the feet, which were painted to resemble skating boots. Many people collected the ballerinas, which came in a range of different coloured tutus.

'The Cries of London', an unusual range, was one of the earliest and it remained in production throughout the life of the company. Based on a series of works featuring street vendors, by Eighteenth-Century artist Frederick Wheatley, the dolls wore the costumes shown in his paintings. Amongst them were Lavender Girl, Cherry Ripe, Flower Girl, Orange Seller, Turnips and Carrots, and Strawberries Scarlet. Each doll wore an authentically-styled full-skirted dress, a frilly cap or hat, and carried a basket of her wares.

The National Costume series, comprising dolls in colourful outfits from around the world, came into being after Peggy was inspired by the beautiful and colourful costume dolls sold in France, comparing them with British dolls available at the time for tourists. Tourists were also fond of the Historical Characters, especially Henry VIII and his wives, Elizabeth I and Nell Gwyn. As with the 'Cries of London' series, costume authenticity was very important to Peggy, and entailed a great deal of research with visits to museums and libraries, and long hours spent in the National Portrait Gallery.

Over the years, dozens of famous personalities in doll form passed through Peggy's hands, but, it must be said, some are some more instantly recognisable than others. Sir Winston Churchill's 'bulldog' expression was captured perfectly, as were the likenesses of Stan Laurel

Peggy Nisbet Sonja the Skater

and Ollie Hardy, but many other characters are more apparent by their costume than their features. Charlie Chaplin, Charlotte Brontë, Judy Garland, Dame Ellen Terry, George Washington, Danny Kaye, Lily Langtry, Jacqueline Kennedy, Queen Victoria and King Tutankhamun are just a few of the dozens of portrait dolls which were issued.

Rexard

Rexard produced a range of basic plastic dolls, all with similar faces, but which were dressed in a wide variety of outfits, both National and Historical. The dolls were distributed from the company's main premises in Worthing, Sussex and packed in boxes, usually triangular, though sometimes square boxes containing a set of dolls were used. They were widely sold in the 1960s/70s at newsagents, confectioners' shops, 'corner shops' and tourist outlets, and were a cheap way of adding a costume doll to a collection. Although the dolls were not of the quality of the Peggy Nisbet dolls, they were still very attractive. Children, in particular, bought them, not to play with but to collect, though they also appealed to adults. Today, there are thousands upon thousands of the dolls around, invariably in good condition – as they weren't intended to be undressed, they tended to stay in their boxes or on a display shelf.

These Rexard dolls were usually made from a hard, thin plastic and stood 7½ or 8½ inches high, depending on the model. They had wigs in various

Rexard Devon Violet Seller

styles and colours, to suit the character, and had painted eyes. Often, dolls bore a tag which read 'Designed by Odette Arden. Made in the British Empire.' The company also distributed other ranges including a series of smaller dolls with rounder faces and sleep-eyes, dressed as policemen, guardsmen and soldiers. Later, softer plastic types appeared.

Rogark

Rogark were a small company based in Wales, and their costume dolls were familiar, especially, to visitors to Scotland and Wales in the late 1950s and throughout the 1960s. The dolls were 7 inches high, made from hard plastic, with distinctive faces featuring rather staring eyes. They were extremely well dressed, the Welsh dolls often wearing a small metal leek brooch, whilst the Scottish dolls came with bagpipes. The company also made a range of miniature dolls, some with bristles instead of legs, and when the tabletop was tapped, the dolls 'danced'. They could also be made to dance when placed on top of a piano – as the notes were played, the dolls twirled.

Shallowpool costume dolls: Dairy maid, Pasty girl, Cream maiden

Shallowpool

This range of dolls in traditional British costume was produced through the 1950s and 1960s, until the late 70s. At first glance they resemble the Peggy Nisbet dolls, although, unlike the latter, no attempt was made to source the small-patterned fabrics and authentic materials. The dolls stood around 8 inches high, although there was a 'Nursery Rhyme' range which was a little shorter; dolls in this were 5–6 inches tall depending on the character. A further range of 'specials', 15 inches high, was also created, though these are rare. The dolls' heads, arms and legs were made from plaster of Paris, which had been poured into latex moulds until set, then attached to a padded wire armature. The faces were beautifully hand-painted, incorporating lots of character, especially in the men folk, and the clothing style had been well-researched. Many of the dolls came with a short poem or

Shallowpool
Cornish Lady

piece of prose, telling about the character they depicted, and most had accessories of one kind or another such as fish, fruit, a barrel, a plate or even a pig, all moulded from plaster of Paris. Creels and baskets were made from wicker.

The dolls were made in Cornwall, as a cottage industry set up by three ladies, Joan Rickarby, Muriel Fogarty and Peggy Pryce, and the majority depicted Cornish characters – smugglers, tin miners, ferrymen, fishermen, various flower and fruit sellers, town-crier, huntsman, cream maiden, morris dancers, china clay miners, pirate captain and a velvet-gowned lady dressed in a riding costume as worn by one of Daphne du Maurier's hero-ines. These costumes reflected all aspects of Cornish history, from workers to gentry. A further range covered historical characters such as Henry VIII and Nelson, while the Nursery Rhyme characters were intended to appeal to youngsters and included Old Mother Hubbard, Little Miss Muffet, Little Bo Peep and Red Riding Hood.

However, the most unusual Shallowpool dolls were those based on notable Cornish folk, for instance Mary Kelynack, a Newlyn fishwife who walked to London and presented Queen Victoria with half a pound of tea. Then there was Jenny Johns, a coal-heaver, celebrated for her achievement of carrying two hundredweight of coal in a basket on her head, and Dolly Pentreath, a lady from Mousehole, who lived till she was 102. Dolly Pentreath's poem read:

Old Doll Pentreath, one hundred ag'd and two,
Deceased and buried in Paul parish too.
Not in the church with people great and high,
But in the church-yard doth old Dolly lie.

One of the most commonly-found of the dolls is the Cornish pasty seller, probably because she was an unusual, yet quintessential souvenir of Cornwall, where tourists enjoy indulging in traditional Cornish pasties filled with meat and vegetables. Holding her pasty in both hands, her verse reads:

Pastry rolled out like a plate
Piled with 'turmut, tates and mate'

Doubled up and baked like fate
That's a 'Cornish Pasty'.

Other ladies with their wares include a Cream Maiden, Milk Maid, Primrose Seller, Violet Seller and Apple Seller. The Apple Seller, with her basket full of rosy apples, has a verse which reads:

Ripe apples need picking when autumn is here,
For making the cider so golden and clear.

Particularly unusual were the various tin miners and china clay workers. The latter were dressed all in white, and carried their candles; whilst amongst the tin miners were men carrying hammers and women Bal Maidens whose job it was to break up the large rocks. The fishermen, smugglers, ferrymen and pirate captains in the Shallowpool range are also very evocative of the region, and in many cases the makers have managed to capture the weathered look of the faces.

Amanda Jane Jinx doll dressed in Wales

Various Makers

Many major manufacturers, such as Roddy, Rosebud, Tudor Rose, Pedigree and Palitoy sold their dolls undressed to tourist concerns for them to dress locally. In addition, individuals living in tourist locations would buy small quantities of the dolls which they would dress at home. Consequently, collectors come across many dolls, often beautifully dressed, but which can't be attributed to their supplier, and which don't appear in the doll company's catalogue. For example, I have a delightful Amanda Jane Jinx doll, dressed in Welsh costume, and on its box it reads, 'By Helene Kay of Conway', stating that the doll's name is Enid, and that she cost 10/6d (53p). Sometimes though, the major manufacturers also produced their own versions of their dolls ready-dressed in Scottish, Welsh or Irish costume, to be sold direct to the shops or to tourist boards and similar outlets.

Various Types of Craze or Cult Dolls

The other way a teenager could buy a doll without appearing strange or childish, was to collect 'cult dolls'. These were quirky types which became all the rage for a year or so – or even a few months – before disappearing from sight. Just as happens today, a toy or doll would suddenly become the must-have of the moment, and amongst the items would be those intended to appeal to teenagers. They included Hug-a-Bugs or Winky dolls, Boudoir types, nightdress/handkerchief holder dolls, and ornamental types such as 'Glooks' and 'Gonks' – most of these items are nowadays derogatively referred to as 'Kitsch'.

Boudoir Types

These dolls with the large 'made-up' eyes, pouty lips and, often, trendy fashions, were perfect for teens to use to ornament their bedrooms. The heads were made from fabric over a hard, moulded shape, while the bodies were cloth over a wire armature. The legs and arms were bendy, and sometimes the dolls featured coloured, wool hair. Usually made in Japan, they were in vogue for several years during the early to mid sixties. Many of them feature a 'gold' pendant in the shape of an open circle. I recall buying mine on a holiday trip to Walton on the Naze. I must have been about 14, and admired the dolls in a shop window. Mum told me that I ought to buy one, as she would look lovely in my room. I needed no second bidding! Today, she is one of my treasured mementoes, and is one of the trendy types in pink felt trousers, a yellow and black striped top, pale pink hair and with large feet encased in black strap sandals. I later bought another, slightly darker in colouring, wearing a straw hat and a yellow top.

Another similar range of dolls wore traditional crinoline-type outfits in coloured satins, with bonnets and parasols. Sometimes these dolls, especially the crinoline types, are referred to as 'Bradley dolls', presumably referring to a maker's name. Many of these dolls are mounted on bases, rather than posed sitting, as my dolls are, and the golden 'Japan' stickers are found underneath the base. It's possible that these Bradley types continued well into the 1970s.

**'Boudoir' type
1960s' dolls**

Gonks looked rather like Beatles!

Glooks, Gonks and Trolls

There were so many crazes in the 1960s; it was definitely a fun era. Glooks were fluffy, oval brightly-coloured creatures with very long hair and large eyes and noses. The idea was to brush the hair into various strange shapes. I still have my red Glook! Gonks were round, fabric creatures, again with big eyes and noses, rather resembling Humpty Dumpty. Sometimes they had a small tuft of hair. However, another sixties' collectable also bore the Gonk name; though sometimes they were called Trolls. These were made from highly polished wood, with oval heads and bodies and arms made from thick stiff string. They had tufts of fluffy hair – I had a set which

Inflatable Hug-a-Bug or Winky doll

looked just like The Beatles. Glooks and Gonks appealed to teens, they were a fun collectable, an acceptable form of a 'doll'.

Hug-a-Bugs

Also known as 'Winky Dolls', these odd, black dolls made their first appearance in the early 1960s, enjoying a revival in the 1970s. They came in many sizes, and the larger ones were inflatable. Young girls used them as a fashion accessory, wearing the dolls by making them 'hug' their arms, legs or handbags! They squeaked when pressed, and featured large winking eyes, which were officially known as 'lenticular', meaning that two images

Libby's milk advert, 1961

were printed on grooved plastic, and depending on how the eye was viewed, it either appeared open or closed. Their mouths were shaped like a large 'O' and sometimes they had a plastic bow on their heads. Often, they had 'gold' earrings in their large looped ears, and wore plastic 'hula' skirts. An advert of the time offered the inflatable kind for 3/11d (19p) plus labels from Libby's evaporated milk, and added, 'The novelty doll of the year. Clings! Winks! Whistles!'

The smaller dolls were made from a firmer plastic, but looked just like their older siblings, and still featured the bent limbs even though they couldn't really grip. They usually had a loop of plastic at the top of their heads so they could be hung up. Sometimes the dolls were given away as fairground prizes. They wore plastic skirts, too. Occasionally, you come across larger models of these dolls made from a hard black plastic. They still feature the distinctive lenticular eyes, and round mouths, and presumably, these too were called Winky dolls.

Nightdress Cases

Some companies, such as Chiltern, produced dolls dressed with long skirts in which a nightdress could be kept. The Chiltern dolls featured a strange moulded body shape, rather like a large bobbin, which went inside the wide, zipped velvet skirt (there were no legs to the doll). They had the head

Chiltern nightdress case doll

used for the large teen dolls produced by the company, with short rooted Saran hair. These dolls came in many different dress colours, including red, black, blue and green.

In the 1960s dolls were also popular when attached to handkerchief cases, or given long full skirts to decorate and hide toilet rolls, telephones and teapots. Women's magazines contained patterns to create the skirts for these, and the dolls were widely sold at garden fêtes and sales of work.

Collection of costume dolls

Chapter 9

Clever Dolls

As manufacturers in the 1960s mastered the techniques of vinyl, they began to realise the endless possibilities with regard to doll design. For the first time they had a material which was completely washable, wouldn't crack or break and was light and hollow, so there was room to install mechanisms – dolls could be allowed to walk, dance or somersault, because if they did fall, they would come to little harm. Companies vied to come out with new and exciting ideas which would make their doll stand out from the hundreds of others which filled the toyshops at the time. Some of these dolls were developed using American technology, such as speech mechanisms. There were so many clever dolls around in the 1960s that I have only been able to include a few – these are some of my favourites (see also Chapter 10).

Baby First Step by Rosebud

Baby First Step

This pretty toddler was issued by Rosebud in 1964, who boasted: 'She walks all by herself!' She was a battery-operated sturdy doll, 17 inches high, very pretty with blonde curly hair and a chubby toddler face. As the instructions stated, 'Baby First Step will sometimes falter and rock before starting to walk, just like a real baby. She is designed to give you many hours of walking fun with just one set of batteries . . . Brush off any lint or dirt from soles of shoes. Baby First Step will automatically stop walking if she is laid on her stomach or back (or if she falls).' The instructions also issue the warning, 'MAKE SURE DOLL'S PANTS ARE KEPT FREE OF LEG JOINTS.' Later, when Mattel took over the company, she was updated and reissued under the Mattel name.

Baby Party

Made by Pedigree, this was quite an expensive doll, retailing at 99/11d (£4.99) in 1969. This happy little baby, 18 inches tall, was extremely clever as she could blow up a balloon, toot a horn, play with party favours (the blow-out kind with a feather on the end!), and even blow bubbles – all done just by clapping her hands together. Baby Party came in a pink dress, complete with party hat, horn, favour, balloon and bubble pipe, and probably because of her price, is quite difficult to find today.

Baby Party by Pedigree

Chatty Cathy

Chatty Cathy had arrived in America in 1959 – her speech mechanism allowed her to repeat many phrases, and she was proving very popular. The Rosebud company applied to Mattel for permission to use the voice mechanism, and in late 1962 issued the first British Chatty Cathy. This doll was completely unlike the American version, which featured an open laughing mouth and lots of freckles. The Rosebud doll was quite bland and rather old-fashioned looking. Nevertheless she proved popular with little girls due to all the things she could say, such as, 'My name is

Three versions of Rosebud Chatty Cathy

Rosebud', 'Let's go to the park', 'I love you Mummy', 'Hold me please', 'I'm very sleepy', 'Do you like my dress?' and 'Let's play a game', eleven sayings in all. Rosebud Chatty Cathy retailed at £5.19.6d (£5.98p).

She stood 21 inches high, and had a soft vinyl face with sleep-eyes, a serious mouth and rooted hair. Her body was of harder vinyl, and the voice mechanism was operated by pulling the ring in the doll's back. The speaker grid could be seen in the chest. Her cotton dress came in various styles and colours, but usually featured white sleeves with a coloured pinafore effect. She was marked 'Rosebud Mattel. Made in England, Pat. Applied For' (Mattel needed to be credited as the voice mechanism was theirs), and was the subject of a major advertising campaign, alongside Rosebud's Wonder Baby (see Chapter 6).

Two years later, Rosebud released another Chatty Cathy; by now the company had been taken over by Mattel, but she was still marked 'Rosebud Mattel. Made in England' on her back, while on her neck was the word 'Rosebud', in script. This new doll featured very unusual black eyes with no pupils, and she had more of a smile with just a hint of teeth. Standing 21 inches high, she was available with various hair styles, some of which featured unusual two-tone shading. She came in a selection of bright and cheerful clothes, such as an almost psychedelic floral dress which was very 1960s and was trimmed with a pink and yellow daisy. Another outfit featured a mini-dress with a striped top, orange skirt, a wide orange daisy-trimmed tie and a jaunty hat, again very much in fashion.

Towards the end of the 1960s, in 1968, yet another version of Chatty Cathy was issued in Britain by Rosebud Mattel. This doll, 21 inches high, had a wide, smiling, open mouth revealing teeth, and there was more of an American feel to her. She had long, very thickly-rooted hair and was dressed in a white top and a blue floral skirt with straps. Her back was marked 'Rosebud Mattel. Made in England'. This third issue of Chatty Cathy bore a very strong resemblance to other Mattel talking dolls.

Also produced in the 1960s was Chatty Baby, a toddler with short hair which was cut in a baby style. This 18-inch doll had a sweet face with a mouth revealing two teeth, and was similar to the American version of the same doll. She wore a red dress with straps over a white top, and the dress was embroidered 'Chatty Baby' near the hem. Chatty Baby had the pull ring speech mechanism, and bore the Rosebud rose on her back. She also came in a larger size, which seems to be harder to find. There were other dolls in the range too, including 'Singing Chatty Cathy' and 'Baby Singing Chatty Cathy' (see Chapter 10 for other Mattel dolls). The Pedigree company were also involved with the marketing of some of the Mattel Chatty Cathy series.

A word of warning comes from an American doll collector, Maggie Gustafson, regarding the random speech mechanisms of these dolls: 'Even though I was a teenager in the 60s, I still got dolls – I just called myself a collector. (And that's my excuse for playing dolls today!) One of the dolls I got was called Charming Chatty, made, I think, by the Ideal Doll Company. The doll had little records that could be inserted into a slot in the side of the doll and would play random sayings when the string was pulled. One day I was demonstrating this to my boyfriend and was embarrassed to have the doll say, "Take me to bed with you!" Gosh, those were more innocent times! I still have the doll, and the ex-boyfriend remains a friend also, even though we grew up and married other people.'

Drowsy

Another clever doll from the Rosebud/Mattel collaboration, this soft-bodied baby spoke in a sleepy voice as she drifted off to the land of nod. The box read: 'I'm a talking sleepyhead! You never know what I'll say next. Just pull my chatty ring.' Drowsy had a distinctive vinyl face with a sleepy look, and apart from her hands, the rest of her was fabric, so she was cuddly and perfect for a child to take to bed. Measuring 15 inches tall, she had short rooted hair and a sweet smile. She dates from 1964, and could speak eleven different phrases with a pull of the ring mechanism, including, 'I'm sleepy' and 'Kiss me goodnight'. Her clever box converted into a rocking cradle. Most commonly found types of Drowsy are the pink spot body fabric version, although others, such as one decorated with cats, exist.

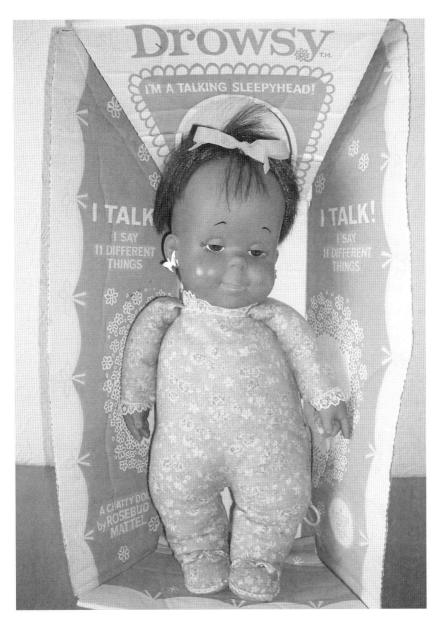

Drowsy by Rosebud/Mattel

Patti Pit-a-Pat by Palitoy

Patti Pit-a-Pat

This delightful, sturdy toddler stood out from the crowd, because she was a little plain; a refreshing antidote to the dozens of blonde-haired cuties of the era. Patti Pit-a-Pat had her short hair cut in a no-nonsense bob, finished off with a slight top-knot, and while her round, pleasant, rather earnest face could not by any stretch of the imagination be called pretty, it was quite striking. Her eyes were of the sleep kind and featured long thick hair lashes. Standing 20 inches high, she was marked 'PM Sales Inc. c1966 Palitoy Made In England 2'.

Patti was battery-operated, and when the switch on her back was turned on, she determinedly stomped along on her large feet. Her head was a soft vinyl, but her body and legs were of a very hard plastic. The advertising blurb read, 'Just slide the button in her back and she walks – all on her own.' Usually Patti wore a plain short-sleeved cotton dress, which came in a variety of bright shades including yellow, pink or red, and which was trimmed at collar and sleeves with white. The dress featured four golden buttons on the bodice.

Tiny Talk

Another talking doll dating from the 1960s was Tiny Talk by Palitoy. Smaller than the Chatty Cathy range, she stood 14 inches high, with vinyl head and arms and a hard plastic body. Wearing a cotton dress with a pink bodice and a blue floral skirt, Tiny Talk had short hair, sleep eyes with long lashes, and a slightly pursed mouth. She was operated by a ring-pull cord and said several phrases in a very refined British accent, including, 'I'm Tiny Talk. I walk and talk', 'Can we play in the park today?', 'Can I wear my hat and coat today?' and 'Are you coming out to play?' Her back was marked, 'Made in England by Palitoy. Pats Pending.'

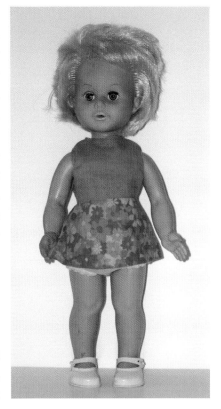

Tiny Talk by Palitoy

Tiny Talker

Dating from 1966, Tiny Talker was a 16-inch high doll from Pedigree, who could say eighteen different things. She had short blonde hair with flick-ups and a top knot, and came dressed in a denim shift with broderie anglaise trimming and red tights. On the front of her shift were a large daisy and a silver Pedigree brooch. She retailed for 85/3d (£4.27)

Tippy Tumbles

One of the most recognisable of the 1960s' dolls, Tippy Tumbles is another of those who have become something of a classic. She was first issued in Britain in 1969 by Palitoy, under licence from the US Remco Industries, and was voted 'Girls' Toy of the Year' at the toy fair.

Her face was not particularly pretty – it was more of a character type, with chubby cheeks and a wide smile, and had a distinctive square appearance. She had fixed, slightly staring, blue eyes, long lashes and

Tiny Talker by Pedigree

Tippy Tumbles by Palitoy

rooted blonde hair. Tippy stood 17 inches high, and had a vinyl head and arms, but her body and legs were made from hard plastic. When undressed, she looked fairly basic, her body was strange due to the odd leg assembly – they were strangely mounted at the hips into square-cut hollows – and her hands were splayed and held palm down. There was little detailing on her feet, just a hint of toes. Five screw-holes in her back bore testament to the fact that a mechanism was within. The doll was marked 'SM Palitoy Remco Ind. Inc. 19©68' on the back of her neck. Her most unusual feature was a 'plug socket' of three small holes in her leg, near her right ankle.

When the doll was sold, she was usually dressed in stretch nylon navy blue tights, held up by narrow elastic straps, which had a small opening above the ankle to correspond with the plug socket. She also wore a red sleeveless top with blue, white and yellow stripes which fastened at the back with the distinctive small metal Palitoy studs.

Tippy Tumbles claim to fame was that she could perform somersaults,

**Tippy Tumbles
by Palitoy**

turning head over heels. She was operated by a battery-box with a long lead and plug attached, and these boxes were cleverly designed to look like handbags. They were made from red or blue hard plastic, and a lever on the top of the bag turned on the mechanism. The plug was then attached to Tippy's ankle and she performed quite impressively. There are still thousands of Tippy Tumbles dolls around, but the boxes are harder to find. In America, there were several versions of the doll, including a clown.

Although she was a child's toy, Tippy Tumbles wasn't really intended

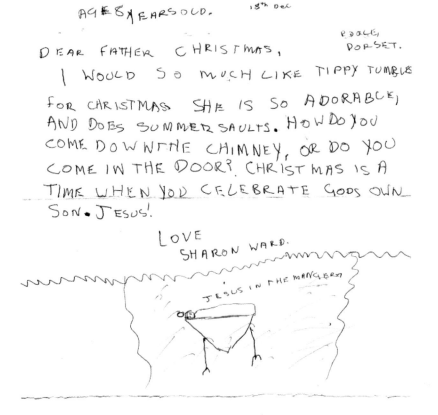

Child's plea for a Tippy Tumbles by Palitoy

to be undressed and played with as a baby doll; this was a performing doll. Consequently, this is probably why so many of these are still found wearing their original clothes and in good condition – they were fun for a while, but then rejected in favour of a more conventional doll.

Although the Palitoy company ceased doll production in the 1980s, it's a testament to the quality of their products that so many of the mechanical types still survive in working order.

Other clever dolls of the 1960s included Talkative Jane (Pedigree), Walk 'n' Talk Poppet (Palitoy), Susie Sing-a-Song (Pedigree), Baby Sparkle Eyes (Pedigree) and Pouting Pretti (Palitoy).

Rosebud Baby First-Step

Chapter 10

American Invasion

Although American dolls had been sold in Britain for years, the 1960s saw a surge in the quantity as several US and British factories came to arrangements to market the dolls over here. In addition, some American concerns set up companies in Britain; it meant that many new lines were introduced, but was also the beginning of the American domination which was to decimate the British doll industry by the 1980s.

The Ideal Toy Corporation, in particular, was responsible for many new and interesting 1960s' lines, which is why it is looked at in depth in this chapter. Many of the dolls sold though other US concerns have already been dealt with under the corresponding British company, including Palitoy and Rosebud. But the biggest giant of all was Mattel.

One of the reasons why the Americans were so successful was that they allocated far more of their budget for advertising and promotion. They were also more professional in their presentation. A report in the magazine *Toys International*, 1965, said, 'Even if the American invasion of Britain was short-lived, it would leave behind it a legacy of professionalism that would never be lost.' In the main, British companies were reluctant to run continual full-scale advertising campaigns, apart from initial launch commercials for major lines such as Sindy, Tressy and Tiny Tears.

Deluxe Toy Co. Ltd./Topper Toys

This American company, affiliated to the US giant Deluxe Reading, was also in Britain, with offices in London and a works at Hayes, Middlesex. Many of their dolls were issued under the Topper brand name, and amongst their 1960s' offerings were two delightful small dolls, both of which are fondly remembered today by doll-lovers – Penny Brite and Suzie Cute.

Penny Brite

An In-Depth Look At A Penny Brite Doll

This little doll, just 8 inches tall, can be easily recognised by her beaming smile and dimples. Penny Brite has painted eyes which look to the left and painted lashes, too. Her rooted hair is short, blonde and curly, and is finished with a red ribbon bow. She is jointed at neck, hips and shoulders and her limbs are rubbery and soft, but unlike many fashion dolls of the time, they will not hold a pose as they do not contain a wire armature.

Penny's most familiar outfit is a red and white pleated short-sleeved dress with a white collar and cuffs. The three white panels on the front of the dress feature blue flower trims. For such a small doll, the dress is surprisingly well-detailed, with top-stitching on the bodice. She also has white flat shoes and was sold packaged in a small plastic carry case. Considering her size, she had quite a lot of markings: on the back of her head it read 'A-9A75 Deluxe Reading Corp. c1963' while her back bore the mark 'Deluxe Reading Corp, Elizabeth NJ, Pat. Pending'.

Various other outfits were available separately; amongst them were 'Singing in the Rain', 'Anchors Aweigh', 'Sunday Best', 'Picnic Treat' and 'Smart Shopper'. Penny Brite also had various accessories such as a schoolroom, complete with a school dress, blackboard, easel, chair and desk, and a beauty parlour which contained a hair-dryer, sink and chair.

Penny Brite by Deluxe Reading

Suzy Cute

An In-Depth Look At A Suzy Cute Doll

This little, rather toothy, charmer is still easily found today. Suzy Cute first appeared in 1965, and was a 6½-inch toddler, made from a very hard vinyl. She represented a toddler, and was a drink and wet doll, so provided plenty of fun for small girls. Her blonde hair was short and straight, and was combed into a side parting, while her fixed eyes, with their plastic lashes, were bright blue. A smiling open mouth revealed two lower teeth.

Suzy's arms were on a kind of spring mechanism, and when you gave her a squeeze, she raised her arms in the air as though asking to be picked up. The back of her neck is marked 'Deluxe Reading Corp. c 1964 27', while on her back it reads 'Made in Hong Kong'. When Suzy was sold, she came in a fine cotton sky-blue short angel top which fastened with a

Suzy Cute by Deluxe Reading

popper at the back, and was decorated on the front by a pink embroidered flower motif on a bow. The hem, sleeves and neck of the angel top were trimmed with narrow white lace. Underneath the top Suzy wore a pair of sky blue knickers edged with white lace.

Plenty of accessories and outfits were available to buy separately, including 'Hop, Skip and Jump' (a playsuit with blue pants and white embroidered dress), 'Honey and Spice' (a yellow and white shift embroidered with ducks), 'Fancy Frills' (a blue party dress with embroidered flowers to celebrate Suzy's first birthday), 'Sweet Dreams' (a pink and white sleep suit), 'Splash 'n' Dry' (a white terry bathrobe trimmed with pink and white, and a nappy) and 'Winter Angel' (a red hooded jacket trimmed with white 'fur' and red leggings).

Toys were available for Suzy, and amongst them was a large, 14-inch x 12-inch, playground which consisted of a swing, seesaw and slide, all in red and yellow plastic. They were mounted inside a frame which formed the playground. It had yellow sides, a green base and a rod along the top to hold the swing and slide in place. Other accessories included a carry case and a wardrobe, a yellow and red dresser which had an umbrella on top, a 'bathinette' (a red bath with a splash-back on a yellow stand with a tray beneath), a yellow cot with plastic animal beads, and smaller items such as bottles, dummies, rattles, brush and comb.

This is a well-made and sturdy little doll that makes a great addition to a collection of similar-sized baby and toddlers. Unfortunately, as with many other American dolls also marketed in the UK, many of the items and accessories for Suzy Cute were not easily available in Britain, but it is certainly worth hunting them out.

A few years before Suzy Cute came on the scene, Deluxe Toy Co. released another Suzy, Suzy Smart. Much taller than Suzy Cute, at 24 inches, she was made from hard plastic with a vinyl head, sleep-eyes and rooted blonde hair. She featured jointed knees so that she could sit at a desk – because Suzy Smart was a schoolgirl. Dressed in a school-time outfit, she came with a desk, chair, blackboard and easel, and really lived up to her name as she could talk – 'she recites, she spells, she adds!'

Similar to several other dolls by various companies at the time, was Baby Tickle Tears, an expression-changing 14-inch baby with rooted fair hair. She had an open mouth to take a dummy, and painted black eyes with tear

Baby Tickle Tears by Deluxe Reading

ducts. When her arms were pulled down, she pouted and cried, but when the button in her tummy was pushed, she smiled and raised her arms. Baby Tickle Tears was marked '38 Deluxe Reading Corp C 1966'.

General Mills

This huge American company, which is still active today, is mainly concerned with foodstuffs. Founded in 1856, it acquired various flour mills and became especially famed for its cereals. In 1965 the company decided to test the waters of the toy market, buying Rainbow Crafts, who were the manufacturers of Play-Doh, and also Kenner. Two years later it bought Palitoy Toys from British Xylonite, following up with the Denys Fisher company in 1970. By doing this it meant that Palitoy could introduce many American lines into the UK, often adapting the doll's design to suit British tastes, but utilising the mechanism or the name, thus dolls such as Tiny Tears, Tippy Tumbles and Tressy came into being.

Ideal

The old, established Ideal Toy Corporation announced it was setting up a British factory in 1967. They went on to release a succession of dolls in the United Kingdom, including several classics, such as Giggles, Crissy, April Showers and Flatsy, which are all very much collected today.

AN IN-DEPTH LOOK AT A FLATSY DOLL

This distinctive little doll really can't be mistaken for anything else, and the name, Flatsy, suits it perfectly! This doll, like most of its siblings, stands

Ideal Flatsy doll

just under 5 inches tall, and is totally flat. In fact, she looks as though she has been run over by a road-roller.

She is made of a rubbery vinyl, and resembles a gingerbread girl with her feet turned out to the side, and her hands with front-facing palms. Flatsy has large, painted, side-glance eyes, a round blob nose and a smiling mouth. Her nylon hair is long; often the hair on these dolls reaches to the ankles. In addition, hair indication lines have been moulded into the plastic under the nylon hair. She is marked 'Ideal 1969 Pat. Pend. Hong Kong' on her back, just above her moulded-on knickers.

The construction is interesting – inside the vinyl are lengths of wire and these enable the limbs, neck and body to be posed in a variety of ways. On the doll are several sets of two pin-holes, occurring on the reverse of the ankles, wrists and head, as well as the back. The purpose of the holes is to attach the doll to a play set. As with the Flatsy dolls, the play sets are flat, resembling a picture and often bearing a frame. Various flat accessories came with the dolls, some quite elaborate, such as a train or car, and these too could be attached to the play set background.

Outfits found on Flatsys varied considerably, from dungarees to PVC coats and from nightwear to party dresses. They wore an assortment of colourful clothes, with a definite sixties feel, and they usually came with hats and shoes, though these tended to soon go missing. Also sold were Boy Flatsys, with shiny moulded hair. As with any popular doll, there were plenty of imitations, but the genuine Flatsys were clearly marked on their backs. They were made by Ideal from the late sixties to the early 1970s.

In America, there were many different Flatsy doll types available, including several with brightly coloured blue, green, pink or purple hair, but these seem more difficult to find in Britain. There were also other sizes; a mini, around 2.5 inches, and a slimmer 'Fashion', which was almost double the height of the standard doll.

AN IN-DEPTH LOOK AT A GIGGLES DOLL

This is one of those instantly recognisable dolls, and was produced by the Ideal Toy Company in 1967. Giggles was promoted as 'The Happiest Doll in the World', and her joyful, cheeky face and infectious laugh endeared her to thousands of children.

Giggles by Ideal

The first things you notice when you look at a Giggles are her large blue flirty-type eyes which move from side to side. The whole face seems animated and alive, and was designed by the famous sculptor Neil Estern who was responsible for many other classic American dolls of the time. He excelled with this one. Giggles is 18 inches tall, and her head is made from soft vinyl, but her body and limbs are of hard vinyl. Her smiling mouth reveals white 'teeth' and there are dimples in both her chubby cheeks. Her eyelashes are painted and her shoulder-length blonde hair is roughly chopped, which causes many collectors to believe that it has been cut by a child, but usually this is not the case. Giggles' hair is meant to look shaggy.

The back of her head is marked 'Ideal Toy Corp. GG-18-H-77' together with the copyright date of 1966, and the doll features an unusual neck joint which allows her head to move sidewards. Once undressed, a grid in Giggles' tummy provides the clue that she is meant to do something, yet there is no battery box, pull string or switch. The secret is in her hands, which are held, slightly splayed, against her side. If the hands are moved apart, she will look from side to side and delightfully giggle. When her hands are brought together she will do it again.

The doll wears a particularly colourful striped outfit, utilising favourite colours of the era – lime, orange, pink and yellow – fashioned as a mini-dress in knitted cotton with matching pants. Inside the dress is a tag which reads 'Giggles Ideal Japan'. She also wears a pair of flat, strappy black sandals, and these are marked 'Hong Kong CM9179' on the soles. Sometimes this doll can be found in different colour schemes or outfits, including a knitted cotton mini-dress similar to the above but in shades of cerise and orange.

Over the years, Ideal issued various dolls in the Giggles series, including a sweet 16-inch bent-limbed baby with short hair, but the doll described here is the kind most commonly found in Britain, and the one which collectors seem to like best. Giggles is a particularly appealing, character-faced little girl and as the box says, 'When Giggles Giggles Everybody Giggles'!

Doll enthusiast Donna Hilson from Essex says, 'I first saw Giggles at a friend's house when I was about six years old and fell in love with her happy expressive face. To me at that age she was big and I remember asking

Giggles by Ideal

**Tearie Dearie
by Ideal**

my mum for her for Christmas but I never did get her. She had hair you could brush, she was the right size for a pram and she giggled when you pulled her arms together. Wow, it was magic to me. How did she do that? I was mesmerised by her and I never came across another one until a few years ago, and all those happy memories of playing with Giggles came flooding back. The one I found was at a boot sale; she was dirty, her hair was matted but the face was happy and smiling, like she was waiting for me to rescue her and take her home at long last. For £1 and quite a few happy hours of cleaning and TLC, she looks lovely, and has pride of place in my collection. She giggles as good as new, too, thanks to instructions I found on the Internet to repair her voice box. I still get the same warm feeling when I look at my Giggles now, and remember playing with her as a child.'

Other dolls produced by Ideal during the sixties included the delightful April Showers. This was a very well made 12-inch high battery-operated baby doll with a character face, painted eyes and open mouth with two lower teeth. When she was seated in a bath of water, her hands would move up and down as she splashed and her head turned from side to side. Amongst the many marks on her back and neck were 'Ideal toy Corp., Made in Hong Kong' and 'c1968 BT/11/H128'. Particularly pretty was Tearie Dearie, dating from 1964. This 9-inch high cutie was a crying, drink and wet baby doll with rooted short blonde hair, styled with a fringe, and originally wore an orange striped dress and matching pants. Her hands and toes were very well modelled, and her lips were of the pale pink so popular in the early 60s.

Another favourite was the range of Thumbelina dolls; in America, there

Toddler Thumbelina by Ideal

were many different types but in the UK, it seems, fewer models were issued. Apparently, the doll was developed by one of Ideal's designers, who adapted a music box mechanism. By changing the gear ratio and spring, he managed to get the doll to squirm. Most of the Thumbelina babies worked by twist knob or pull cord, and would shiver, shake or move in various ways. Thumbelina, 16 inches high, 1962, and Tiny Thumbelina, 14 inches, also 1962, were soft-bodied with vinyl head and limbs, and wriggled and turned their heads when the mechanism, a knob in the back, was activated. Thumbelina was similar to, and worked in a similar way, to a doll made by Rosebud called 'Wonder Baby' (see Chapter 6).

Newborn Thumbelina, 1968, was sold with her own rocking cradle. Just 9 inches long, dressed in orange tights and a white top, this baby rocked her own cradle. The instructions read: 'Place the crib on any flat, smooth surface. Pull the string, on Thumbelina's back, as far as it will go; then lay the string untangled in the crib. Rest Thumbelina's head on the pillow; then tuck her hands into the sides of the crib and newborn Thumbelina rocks herself to sleep. Thumbelina rocks her crib when she's on her tummy, too, (but don't forget to tuck her hands in the crib.)'

Ideal Crissy

Toddler Thumbelina, 9 inches high, came dressed in assorted costumes including a bright pink dress, a yellow dress and trousers, or in a turquoise and orange 'Indian princess' outfit, and was on either a rocking-horse or in a baby walker. Pulling the string caused the doll to move, making the horse rock or the baby walker trundle around. Others, such as Wake-Up Thumbelina, date from the 1970s.

Perhaps, though, of all Ideal's dolls, the Crissy series is the most famed. Crissy was introduced in 1969, so only just makes it into this book. She was a hair-growing doll, with a very distinctive and attractive face; her dark, pupiless eyes were dramatic and her wide smile and high cheekbones gave her a very animated expression. Crissy was a teen doll, 17½ inches high, jointed at neck, hips and shoulders, and was marked 'Ideal Toys Corp. c 1968 Hong Kong QH/17/H120' on her neck and 'c1969 Ideal Toy Corp SH-18' on her bottom. Initially, she wore a tangerine-coloured lacy dress with long sleeves and a ribbon trim at neck, teemed with orange low-heeled shoes. During the 1970s, Crissy was joined by many other members of her family and friends, such as Velvet and Cinnamon.

Mattel

Mattel entered with a bang in 1967 when it acquired Rosebud. For several years previously, the two companies had worked together with Rosebud using much of the American technology (see Chatty Cathy). Other companies, too, were using Mattel mechanisms. However, much more than being just another company selling a variety of dolls, Mattel had something no other company had – Barbie!

Barbie, as we saw in Chapter 3, was the brainchild of Ruth Handler, who had based the teen doll on a German creation, which in turn was founded on a Bild Lilli cartoon. Ruth called her creation Barbie after her young daughter.

A 1967 *Hobbies Annual* gift supplement contains a Barbie section which reads, 'America's most popular (and certainly the most

Early 1960s' Barbies by Mattel

Barbie and Ken by Mattel

heavily advertised) range of fashion dolls, has recently been introduced into Europe with amazing success. Barbie, her MOD cousin Francie and her younger sister Skipper, are a range of beautifully made dolls with the most exclusive wardrobes yet seen. Barbie and Francie can wear each other's clothes, so start with either doll and add-to as you go along. All models supplied with a pedestal stand.'

The two types of Barbie doll advertised in the catalogue were 'Barbie the Model' and 'Barbie the Teenage Model' (which was a slightly more basic doll, and didn't have the jointed knees.) Both dolls were 11½ inches

Skipper by Mattel

Tender Love unjointed doll by Mattel

tall. Barbie the Model featured a blonde bob and wore a blouse-top swimsuit. She sold for 28/11 (£1.44). Barbie the Teenage Model, an auburn-haired doll with a bubblecut, wore a red swimsuit and retailed at 22/11 (£1.14)

Likewise, there were two models of Francie, who was more expensive than Barbie, the de luxe version being 40/3 (£2.02), while even the teen version, at 33/- (£1.65), was dearer than the de luxe Barbie. Skipper, 9 inches tall, came in two versions as well, at similar prices to her sister Barbie.

Amongst the attractive Barbie outfits were 'Concert in the Park', 'Debutante Ball', 'Fashion Luncheon', 'Red Flare', 'Evening Gala' and 'Fun 'n' Games', selling at various prices, often dearer than the dolls themselves. Many of the costumes were very sophisticated, and some were stunning. Barbie was a fashion icon. By contrast, Skipper's outfits were more suited to a younger girl – here were 'Dog Show', 'Learning to Ride' and 'Junior bridesmaid'.

Sharon White, a doll-lover from Dorset, remembers, 'I had one of the 1968/69 Barbie dolls in her swimming costume which I've still got, and I thought she was wonderful although she had a completely different look to her than my cherished Sindy.'

Mattel issued other play dolls in Britain in the late 1960s, including an interesting range of rubbery vinyl dolls with pleasant, smiling faces, which were completely unjointed. They were perfect for smaller children as they were so cuddly. In addition, they produced dolls containing various mechanisms (see Chapter 9 for Chatty Cathy), such as Timey Tell, a 17-inch tall girl with painted eyes, who wore a large watch. When the dial was turned and the string was pulled, the doll told the time indicated on the watch.

Ideal Tearie Dearie

Mattel Timey-Tell

Chapter 11

Retro Dolls

As we've seen, the 1960s was a strong decade; it was the decade when it was cool to be British! For a few short years, Britain was seen as a major influence in terms of fashion, music and the arts. Many of the styles we wore then have disappeared – although they still reappear in slightly different guises every once in a while – but the 'Sixties Look' is still considered chic. Consequently, many dolls are produced nowadays wearing 1960s' fashions; often, these are dolls by major designers such as Robert Tonner, Jan McLean and Doug James. Sometimes they are dolls representing 1960s' characters, such as Twiggy, The Beatles or Andy Warhol. And sometimes, surprisingly, dolls are issued for collectors which are replicas of the dolls children would have played with in the sixties – a classic case must be the porcelain Sindy doll, issued in 2007 by Danbury Mint, who is dressed in the 'Weekenders Outfit'.

Barbie

Over the years Barbie has paid plenty of homage to the 1960s, whether reviving her iconic sixties' outfits, or appearing in outfits influenced by sixties' style.

One of the most iconic Barbie costumes was 'Solo in the Spotlight', issued in 1960, and in 1995, Mattel decided to re-release the outfit, modelled on a vintage-style Barbie which captured the essence of the original doll. The outfit consists of a tight black strapless sheath gown, long black gloves, pink scarf and pearl necklace. Since then, Mattel have re-issued other Barbie classics. She also appeared as 'Groovy Sixties Barbie' in a blue miniskirt, trendy white 'baker's boy' hat and a glorious faux fur cerise pink jacket, but perhaps the most interesting of the sixties-themed Barbies is the Star Trek issue of 1996. Here Barbie dresses in her

Barbie 'Solo in the Spotlight' reproduction by Mattel

engineering officer get-up – a red mini-dress with black trim, while Command Officer Ken sports a yellow and black uniform. The set was issued to mark the 30th anniversary of the *Star Trek* programme.

Barbie 'Feeling Groovy' by Mattel

Beatles

The Beatles seem just as popular today as they were back in the 1960s, although most of the Beatles 'dolls' which appear are really figurines. Amongst the doll-like figures were a set created by Applause in 1987. These were ultra-large, at 22 inches each, and came with their instruments. Being soft-bodied they were quite floppy and needed to be supported on metal stands. Various ranges of figures, such as sets from the *Yellow*

**Beatles (Paul)
Yellow
Submarine**

Submarine cartoon were issued, but they seemed to be more caricature than authentic likeness. Surprisingly, there were also many different styles of Beatles-themed Russian matrioshka wooden dolls.

Betsy McCall

This is another classic doll, this time originally from the 1950s, where she began life as a paper doll. In the 1960s, she was issued in plastic doll form

**Kitty Collier by
Robert Tonner**

by the American Character Co., and in the 2000s, after being taken over by Tonner/Effanbee, amongst Betsy's retro fashions was a delightful mini-dress decorated with a Piet Mondrian print design. The colourful geometrical Mondrian designs were particularly popular in the 1960s after Yves Saint Laurent created a shift dress inspired by them. Betsy's white shift, with its blue, red, black and yellow abstract design is eye-catching.

Candy

Candy, an 18-inch teen girl made by Charisma, appeared in 2008 as 'Groovy Girl' – a hip sixties' chick. The beautiful doll, with long blonde hair, was articulated, not only at the usual joints but at knees and elbows too, so she could be posed in all kinds of ways. Amongst Candy's three sixties' outfits was 'Flower Power', a vivid blue, orange and purple swirling op art design mini-dress with a matching hair scarf. She teamed her outfit with a fashionable pair of white knee-high go-go boots. Her other outfits were 'Mod', which was a zingy pink metallic mini-dress, and 'Paisley' – faux brown suede flares and a cape, together with an orange paisley shirt.

Kitty Collier

The Kitty Collier range by US designer Robert Tonner usually concentrates on the 1950s, but has also produced some outfits with a sixties' theme to suit the 10-inch size 'Tiny Kitty' doll. The outfits include the archetypal two-tone shift dresses – in black and white or red and white – 'Kitty a Go-Go' and 'Mod Togs', as well as a further selection called 'Kit and Caboodle'. Two-tone dresses were all the rage in the 1960s.

Lollipops

The Lollipops dolls are a fun range, which were created by Australian doll designer Jan McLean in 2001. They appear as large 26-inch por-celain editions, as well as in a range

Lollipops by Jan McLean, Lulu

Lollipops by Jan McLean, Pippi La Poo

of 12-inch vinyl fashion dolls. All the dolls have 'kooky' sixties faces, with eyes rimmed with plenty of kohl, and pale pouty mouths. The costumes are very much sixties-influenced, with lots of ultra-short minis, long boots and colourful tights in evidence. The porcelain versions, in particular, are superb with long, long legs and brilliant colour clothing in zany designs.

Each doll represents a different country; two of the most popular are Lulu (London) and Pippi La Poo (Paris). Lulu wears an ultra-short black leather mini, tight black jumper, purple and black stockings and platform shoes. She has long purple hair. Pippi is dressed in black hot pants, black and white striped top and matching stockings and a purple beret. Amongst the others in the series is Bebe of Barbados, dressed in a sizzling hot pink mini. Her spiky hair is bright green. Sassy, a leather-clad beauty from Sydney, has long pink hair, while Scandinavian redhead Nicole is stunning in a white lace micro-mini. Many different costumes are available separately to fit the smaller vinyl versions of these stunning dolls.

Sindy

This beautiful representation of a 1960s' Pedigree Sindy was issued in 2006 by Danbury Mint. She is stunning, and stands 12 inches tall, just like the original doll. However, unlike the original, this Sindy is made from delicate bisque porcelain rather than vinyl. She wears the classic Sally Tuffin and Marion Foale 'Weekenders' outfit of blue jeans, red, white and blue

Sindy BA Cabin Crew in 1967 'paper' uniform

Porcelain Sindy by Danbury Mint 2006

striped long-sleeved top, white sneakers and a red hair-band.

British Airways produced a range of 'retro' Sindy dolls recently, which represent aircraft cabin crew from various eras. The 1960s are portrayed by two dolls: one is Sindy dressed in a navy 1960s' BOAC air stewardess uniform, the other is a delightful copy of the 1967 'paper dress', which was worn at the time by stewardesses on flights between New York and the Caribbean. The dress is white and decorated with large flowers, and Sindy also wears a flower in her hair.

Twiggy

Twiggy was *the* face of the sixties, and so, with all the nostalgia dolls around, it is no surprise that several companies are still releasing dolls in her image. In 2001, Franklin Mint made an outstanding version, standing

Twiggy by Franklin Mint

**Twiggy by
Franklin Mint**

16 inches high and created from porcelain. The likeness to Twiggy was amazing, from the long lashes to the boyish haircut, and the outfit itself was stunning – a psychedelic trouser suit teamed with op art jewellery and purple shoes. Other outfits were available to buy separately, such as a white mini trimmed with silver rings, while a large black and white op art trunk could be purchased to hold the doll, clothes and accessories.

Other Twiggy dolls of the 2000s include a 10-inch high Twiggy by Medicom Toys, which is another excellent representation. This doll has

moulded hair, and wears a typical black and white mini-dress teamed with a wide scarlet low-slung belt and pink-spotted white tights. The same company also made a 'Little Twiggy' doll in a choice of outfits.

Warhol

Andy Warhol was very much part of the 1960s' scene; his design of Campbell's soup cans appeared on posters, cards and clothing through-out the decade, as well as much of his other work, such as his celebrity paintings.

Many years later, in 2000, Merry Makers Inc. issued a soft doll featuring Andy Warhol. This soft cloth, limited edition 15-inch collector's doll was boxed to show the artist seated, wearing jeans, a black leather zip jacket, trainers and, of course, a black jersey bearing a Campbell's soup can design.

Andy Warhol by Merry Makers Inc.

Willow and Daisy

The Knickerbocker Willow and Daisy range of 1960s-influenced dolls first appeared in 1999. The dolls and most of the fashions were designed by Doug James and Laura Meisner and embodied all that was great in the sixties – there was a plethora of PVC, ultra short skirts, kooky get-ups, floaty fabrics and, of course, long tight boots. Some of the fashions were way over the top, but they were fun and colourful. Today the dolls are

**Willow in
'Ladybug
Concert' by
Knickerbocker**

becoming extremely collectable as they were discontinued in 2002, although a further, associated range – Gabby and Violet – was issued in 2007.

Amongst the typical 1960s' styles were 'Ladybug Concert' – an obvious Beatles' tribute, 'Rock and Roll' which was a psychedelic hippie trouser suit and 'Piccadilly', a lemon 'Dolly Rocker' dress with wide, sheer floral-print sleeves gathered at the cuff.

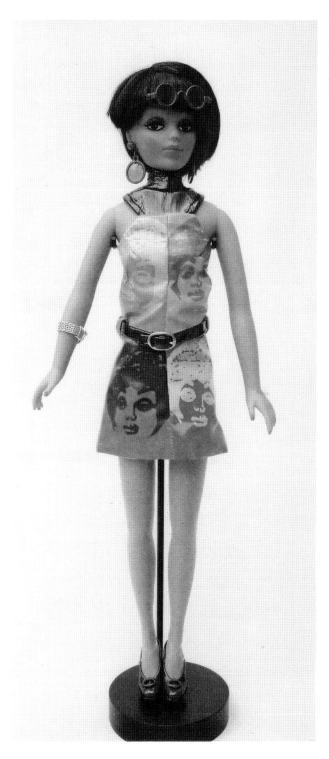

Daisy in 'An Art Opening with Andy and Edie' by Knickerbocker

Other dramatic and colourful styles were a red PVC suit with red thigh-length boots, sported by Daisy and called 'Trafalgar Square' and the spectacular 'Carnaby Street', a lime green and lemon PVC mini with translucent panels. The most unusual of all the outfits was entitled 'An Art Opening with Andy and Edie' – a reference to Andy Warhol and his muse, Edie Sedgwick – which featured Daisy in a vivid Warhol print dress with a high neck and cutaway shoulders. Her black hair was styled in a short geometric cut, and a pair of large turquoise disc earrings completed the look.

Daisy in 'Carnaby Street' by Knickerbocker

Chapter 12

Open the Box?

Many of the 1960s' dolls, especially the fashion types, have been stored in their boxes all these years, giving collectors a wonderful opportunity to obtain a doll with plenty of providence, as well as, often, a mint and unplayed-with item.

Unlike today, most of the 1960s' play dolls were sold in cardboard boxes with lift-off lids, or with open fronts which made the doll easily accessible. Today's dolls are frequently sold in sealed cellophane boxes, with numerous plastic clips and twist wires holding the doll in place, and often the hair is sewn to the backing card – in other words, it is practically impossible to remove the doll without ruining the packaging.

However, some designers, such as Tonner, Doug James, Jan McLean and Franklin Mint are selling their dolls in lift-off top sturdy boxes, and the dolls are secured inside with ribbons. This means the doll can be taken out and displayed, then replaced once more. In this day and age, many collectors prefer their dolls to be mint and boxed, but there can be a downside, and it is something to always bear in mind. In theory, by buying a mint in-box doll you will be getting perfection – but you should always check that the doll hasn't been removed, because a displayed doll could develop faded patches from sunlight, get dusty, have been exposed to damp or have lost some accessories.

Unfortunately, the cardboard boxes can stain the dolls or their outfits, by a reaction of the constituents of the cardboard or dye from the inks. Many older dolls were fastened by elastic bands, and over time these can turn sticky and leave a glutinous mess on the doll. Metal press studs on clothing can cause green marks to appear on the doll's body, staples used in the box construction can produce rust marks on a doll or her clothing, while twist ties can stain or leave grooves or rust marks on limbs. Red clothing is apt to transfer dye onto a doll's body over time.

Plastic and vinyl are prone to certain erratic changes depending on the mix, such as causing 'melt marks' which appear around the joints of some dolls, while some of the 1960s' vinyls can develop blue staining, seen around the eyes, white or brown spots, or a white powdery mildew which forms on the surface of the vinyl and over the eyes.

Dolls from the early part of the 1960s usually came in cardboard boxes, which sometimes bore hand-written labels stating the doll's size, hair and dress colour. Many of these boxes were prettily decorated with nursery characters or perhaps with a drawing or photograph depicting the actual doll. Often the artwork was so attractive that the box was saved, even by children who would normally discard it without a second thought. This can be a bonus for the collector who happens along later. The later 1960s saw open-fronted boxes becoming fashionable, often with a cellophane panel to protect the doll, and shop owners approved of these because their displays could be made more attractive, and a doll could be viewed without removing her from her box.

Even so, many manufacturers continued to use traditional, closed boxes because they provided more protection against accidental knocks and, unlike cellophane, didn't tear so easily. Sometimes, collectors are lucky enough to find 1960s' dolls in boxes, still with their leaflets, tags and brochures – these are priceless to anyone wishing to discover more about their doll's history. Particularly exciting are leaflets detailing the working mechanism of the doll, or colour catalogues of outfits and accessories.

It's important though, to remember that cardboard boxes are not ideal storage containers, and they should be well padded with acid-free tissue paper. Dolls should be kept in even temperatures, not in a loft or garage where they might suffer blazing hot and icy cold conditions over the space of a few months. Never wrap plastic dolls in plastic bags or bubble wrap, and keep them well away from coloured plastic – many a coloured supermarket carrier bag has transferred its design to a doll's body!

However, we must put things in perspective – with all types of collectables there is a risk, and provided we regularly check our dolls, keep them dust free and away from bright sunlight, there should be no problem. The most important thing is always to check a doll's condition before you buy, to ensure that the previous owner has looked after it and kept it in an acceptable condition. Perhaps it might make purists shiver, but often it is better to remove a doll from the box, put her on display and store the box separately, which means that not only can the doll be regularly checked, her owner will also have the pleasure of being able to hold her and examine her, although, of course, removal from the box might well lower the doll's value.

Cleaning and Caring for 1960s' Dolls

Although to many of us, the sixties don't seem so far away, they were almost fifty years ago! Consequently, the majority of 1960s' dolls we find today won't be in pristine condition – they will have been played with, loved or even mistreated by children over the decades.

Often, we will come across a doll, perhaps at a boot sale or jumble sale, which we would love to include in our collections – but it is much the worse for wear. Many people get a great deal of enjoyment from restoring a grimy, bedraggled doll back to, if not perfection, at least to respectability.

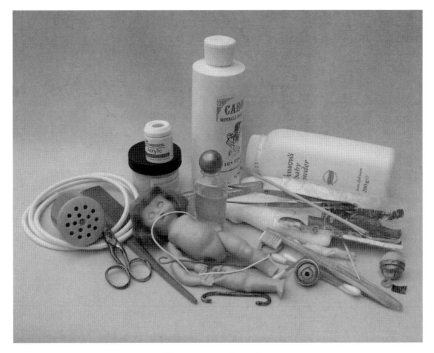

Cleaning and caring

There is a feeling of satisfaction to know that you have rescued a doll which might otherwise have been earmarked for the rubbish heap, and you will have preserved a slice of doll history.

When you have found your vinyl doll, examine it carefully to see if it has any identifiable stains, or if it is just generally dirty. Sometimes, the hair will be matted or eyes might be missing their lashes, while if it's a mechanical doll, it might not be working. Stains you might encounter include ballpoint pen scribble, felt-tip pen, computer ink or other coloured marks (often left when dolls are stored in coloured carrier bags); make-up and nail varnish; brown tint caused by cigarette smoke; mould and mildew or marks left by sticky tape.

Many times it is just a question of a general tidy-up; smoothing the doll's hair, adding a ribbon or two, changing her dress or doing a few running repairs. If the doll is in the original outfit but you wish her to wear something else, it's a good idea to either put the new dress over the top, or to store the original outfit, suitably labelled, so that you can redress her if you wish. Dolls' clothes of this period normally hand-wash well, though beware of red as it tends to run (see Chapter 5).

Ballpoint, Coloured Pen and Ink Blobs

Unfortunately, children love to draw on vinyl dolls because the smooth surface helps the ballpoint ink to freely flow. Dolls become adorned with inky beauty spots, freckles, tattoos or just general scribble. Recently, a collector I know found a doll with the owner's name written in large letters across its forehead, in black felt-tip pen. She removed it successfully, using the method explained here.

You need to buy a product for curing acne, sold as a non-greasy cream. However, before you embark, please be aware that it is a long process; it can take several weeks – sometimes even longer. On the other hand, if you are lucky, one application might be enough – it all depends on the type of ink, the colour of the ink, the intensity of the scribble and how hard the child pressed with the pen.

Spread a layer of the cream onto all the ink spots and scribbles using a cocktail stick or skewer, then put the doll somewhere out of the way and

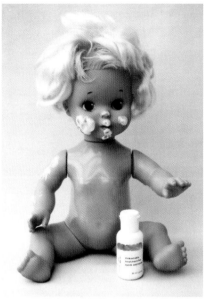

Using acne cream to remove ink from a doll

forget about her for a week. During this time the cream will dry and cake, but will easily come off with a damp cloth, and with a bit of luck, the marks will have faded considerably. In some cases they will have vanished, as if by magic. Just one note of warning – if you use the cream on painted eyes, lips or cheeks, be aware that it might cause fading. If your vinyl doll is a valuable or treasured doll, then it is always wise to try the cream on a part of the doll, such as her bottom, or the sole of her foot, where it won't show if it does cause fading to the vinyl or an adverse reaction.

You might well have to repeat the application process again, maybe several times, but it's a question of patience. Eventually, the cream will shift the majority of the stains, and your doll will have an unblemished skin. I have also used this product on dolls badly stained by black computer ink, felt-tip pens and coloured marks made by plastic carrier bags. (If a doll rests against a carrier bag for any length of time, especially if the bag is damp, you could end up with a doll bearing the name of a supermarket across her face.) Often though, carrier bag marks can be shifted using a mild kitchen cleanser. Interestingly, in warmer countries such as America and Australia, people who use the acne cream method find that if they apply the cream to the doll, then place the doll in the sunlight for a couple of hours (wrapping the doll in a towel, just exposing the treated part), the ultra-violet light seems to react favourably with the cream causing the stain to vanish much more quickly. It's worth trying this in Britain on a rare hot, sunny day!

Naturally, collectors have their own favourite methods for removing ballpoint and similar marks. Some use methylated spirits, car upholstery cleaner or even toothpaste. Another favoured method is butter, which is rubbed into the stain and left for a while to 'lift' it.

Cigarette Smoke

Cigarette smoke is very bad for dolls of all kinds – the vinyl will develop an ugly yellow-brown tint if exposed to smoke for long periods, and the hair will discolour. Usually, a gentle wash in mild soap (see washing section) is all that is needed to brighten up the doll, and it is surprising to see how much of the yellow/brown residue is removed by the damp cloth. The doll's hair will also need washing. Smoke also discolours the doll's clothing and so it will need laundering with the appropriate stain removal products. In severe cases, the doll might still smell strongly of cigarette smoke (see smells).

Cosmetics

It's great fun for children to use make-up products on their dolls, especially on those large sixties' teens. They enjoyed glamorising them with lipstick, eyeshadow and nail polish. Sometimes, children have used play make-up which is relatively easy to remove by wiping with a damp cloth, while the polish can be peeled away. Do check though before you begin that the doll wasn't one of those which were *meant* to have nail polish or eyeshadow!

You might well find, however, that the child has been raiding mum's make-up bag, in which case the cosmetics will take slightly longer to remove. Even so, they shouldn't be too much of a problem. If the make-up is heavily caked because the child has become carried away, and layered it on with a trowel, then remove what you can with tissue. If the doll's lips have become gummed up with lipstick, first remove as much as possible using a cocktail stick to remove the gunge between her lips. You will need some kind of grease-shifting product to remove the rest: make-up remover, cold cream, washing-up liquid, mild liquid cleanser or the gel used by mechanics to clean greasy hands can all be tried, but don't use anything abrasive. Often, if you rub soap into the stain, then rinse it off, it will remove lipstick or blusher. Be careful when removing eyeshadow, as the cleaning products could harm the doll's eyes. Use a cotton bud and acetone-free nail polish remover to remove nail polish.

Mould

Mould can be difficult to remove, especially if it has been on the doll for a long while, as it 'eats' into fabrics and vinyl. The white powdery mould can normally be wiped off, but otherwise try one of the chlorine-free proprietary products sold for removing mould from fabric. It's best to try just a little first, in a place on the doll where it won't show. If the mould spots are faint, they will often shift using a mild liquid kitchen cleanser or pure baby soap.

Mud

Dry mud should just brush off, and if it is a light coating it can be washed off with soapy water. Sometimes it is ingrained into the plastic, in which case you might need to use a mild liquid kitchen cleanser. Don't use any abrasive products as they will scratch the vinyl.

Re-jointing

Sometimes, a doll's legs or arms will become loose, or even drop off. Unlike the 1950s' dolls, very few 1960s' dolls had their limbs attached with elastic, though some of the early sixties' types, especially the hard plastic, *did* still use this method. The easiest way to rethread these is to use a hooked piece of wire or a crochet hook to pass a length of looped elastic (a rubber band for small dolls) through the joint holes in the body, attaching each limb in turn by its hook.

Vinyl dolls often have push-fit joints, which can pop out of their sockets; these can normally be pushed back without too much trouble, but if they won't go back, try holding the top of the joint over a steaming kettle for a minute or two to soften the vinyl before inserting it into the socket. Dolls with more complicated fastenings, such as Tiny Tears, who have ball joints, are probably best mended by a doll hospital.

Smells

One of the worst smells a doll can attract is camphor from mothballs. In fact, it's detrimental to hard plastic dolls, and is believed to trigger hard plastic disease (see my book *British Dolls of the 1950s*). Cigarette smoke is another culprit. Washing the doll using a mild lemon-scented cleanser can be tried, before leaving it near an open window (or even in the garden in the shade) for a few days, will sometimes do the trick, but some smells, particularly camphor, might take much longer to remove. Other ideas include immersing the doll in (unused!) cat litter, scented sawdust or pot pourri – but it could take months before the doll is fresh, as the smell seems to permeate the vinyl.

A tip passed on to me recently is to place a smelly doll inside a closed box together with a small pudding basin filled with bicarbonate of soda, and leave them for a few days. The bicarbonate should absorb the smell.

Sticky Tape/Chewing Gum/Glue/Sticking Plaster

Dolls frequently bear sticky marks from price labels, tape or sticking plasters (children apply the latter to 'injured' dolls), whilst I have often seen long lengths of plaster used to hold on legs or disguise cracks. The best way to remove these is to use one of the proprietary products sold to remove these marks from plastics and china. Neat washing-up liquid sometimes works, too.

Stubborn Stains

Sometimes, when all else fails, drastic methods need to be used. I heard of one vinyl doll which was so badly ingrained with dirt that she would not come clean with any of the usual methods. Her owner just couldn't think what to do, so finally decided on a 'kill or cure method' – she immersed the doll in a bucket filled with a solution of a biological washing powder, and weighted her down with a lid so that she remained below the water surface. The doll was left soaking for a week, and was then retrieved, gleaming! It is not recommended that this is tried on a special or valuable doll, though, as almost certainly the vinyl will fade to a certain extent, but it may be worth bearing in mind for really dirty dolls which would other-wise be binned.

Washing

When vinyl dolls were developed, one of their most acclaimed properties was washability – they could be dunked in the bath. So, in theory, cleaning a 1960s' vinyl doll should not be difficult, but there are certain things to take into account; firstly, and rather obviously, a doll will get wet when immersed in water. Why does this matter? Well, water will soak into the doll's joints, and not only will you end up with a doll who leaves damp patches for a week or so (because dolls take a long time to dry completely), but if it doesn't dry out properly, the doll could develop mould and eventually rot or get smelly. In addition, water soaking the eyes can damage the mechanism, and can also loosen glue which holds in the lashes. It can make the pupils cloudy, too.

So, although it takes longer, it is usually best to wash the doll bit by bit, wiping and rinsing as you go. Fill two bowls with warm water, and add a mild liquid soap product to one, such as that used to bathe babies. Begin washing the doll, using a white cloth and ensuring that it is not dripping with water, then rinse using another cloth. Start with the face, and use a cotton bud for the ears, and crevices around nose and mouth. You can also use a damp bud for the eyes and lids.

Dry using a white towel (coloured flannels and towels can stain plastic), before moving onto the next section, working down the body before turning the doll over to wash the back. For really dirty marks, try rubbing the cloth or a soft toothbrush onto a bar of pure soap, and then working the soap into the marks before rinsing. If they still won't shift, then use a mild kitchen cleanser liquid (nothing abrasive) and apply that. Whatever you use, rinse well, because otherwise a residue will be left which can turn white over time. It's amazing how easy it is to miss a bit, and it's much easier if you work near a window or even in the garden. Some people recommend massaging a drop or two of baby oil into a vinyl doll to impart a sheen.

Washing Hair

Although vinyl dolls have rooted hair, which means it shouldn't easily fall out, it still is best to avoid washing the hair unless it is really dirty, because however careful you are, the hair will often lose much of its gloss and is likely to become 'flyaway'. Obviously, though, if the hair is dirty, or if it is matted, tangled or sticking up on end, then something needs to be done to get your doll looking respectable once more. Wrap the doll in a towel, so that she doesn't get unnecessarily wet, and pour enough lukewarm water onto the hair to make it wet, trying to avoid getting water into her eyes. Hot water should never be used on a doll's hair, as it can set or melt the fibres – the only exception is when restyling the head of a Barbie or similar, and you deliberately permanently set the hair with boiling water, but this is very drastic!

Using a mild shampoo, place a dab onto the hair, lather it well (hopefully the lather will turn dirty as the grime is washed off), then rinse until the water runs clear. You can, at this stage, just allow the hair to dry, but normally it is best to add conditioner to help smooth the nylon fibres; fabric conditioner works well, or you can use the conditioner you use on your own hair. Work it well into the hair without tangling it. Sometimes a doll's hair is so badly matted that you will need to put a plastic bag over the doll's scalp and leave the conditioner to work its magic for at least twenty-four hours. If the hair is really clumped and snarled, you might have to leave for longer.

Usually though, you can rinse the conditioner out after a few minutes before patting the hair dry with a towel, smoothing it into shape and then allowing it to dry naturally. It's important not to use a hairdryer, or leave

Ribbons and trims

the doll near a heat source, as the nylon hair might melt. Once dry, divide the hair into small sections then, working downwards from the ends to the roots, comb the strands until they are straight. This is a slow process, but it's very satisfying to see a head of glossy hair emerge from the tangles. Then style the doll's hair – many of the sixties' vinyls had long hair, so either just comb it straight or form plaits, bunches or ponytails, securing them with ribbons or hairstyling nylon bands. It's not a good idea to use ordinary elastic bands on the hair as they can go sticky. Dolls which originally had curly hair can have it set using rollers or pipe-cleaners which you spray with water, or use a setting lotion. Don't use heated tongs or rollers as they will ruin the doll's hair.

What Should we Collect?

The dolls mentioned in this book cover a huge variety of types and styles, and unless you are fortunate enough to own a really large house, you are unlikely to be able to collect them all.

As with every branch of collecting, the most important piece of advice is 'buy what appeals' – don't buy a doll you hate, just because you think it is collectable. The majority of 1960s' dolls are inexpensive at present, though there are notable exceptions such as Sasha, some Sindys and Barbies, and a few of the more sought after baby dolls. People collect for different reasons; lots of sixties' collectors are seeking to replace their child-hood dolls, while others are interested in certain aspects such as the fashions of the period.

A themed 1960s' collection is a good idea – maybe concentrating on speaking dolls, such as the Chatty Cathy type, mechanical dolls like Tippy Tumbles or, if space is limited, small dolls which will fit on a bookcase. The large fashion teens are fun to collect, and are very glamorous in their high heels and seamed stockings, while Sindy reflects the clothing of the later sixties era. You could aim for examples of the 'classics' – Sasha, Tiny Tears, Babykins and Amanda Jane, or you might find you are attracted to costume dolls.

Whichever you go for, try to buy the best example you can afford, make sure the doll's hair hasn't been cut, that fingers aren't nibbled and the doll

Roddy Toddler girl

isn't scuffed. Seek out original outfits, as it is always interesting to have these with the doll, even if you prefer to sew or knit for the dolls yourself, maybe using 1960s' patterns. Finally, never buy a doll just because you feel she is of a kind which should be represented in your collection. There is nothing worse than having a doll you dislike, with a face like the back of a bus, glaring at you, however collectable she might be.

The 1960s was a fun decade – a recent survey showed it to be the favourite decade amongst adults. It was 'way out', 'groovy' and 'fab'. Those of us lucky enough to be sixties' teenagers will always remember the mad fashions, fluctuating hemlines, eye-dazzling colours, funky make-up and kinky boots. Unlike the 'make do and mend' and 'scrimp and save' philosophy of the 1950s, as the sixties progressed, people became richer, and their outlook changed. Goodness, by 1966, I was earning a mind-blowing £6.7.6d (£6.38) per week! There was money to spend, not only on necessities, but on frivolities too, and, once the toy manufacturers realised this, dolls became ever more realistic and talented – the next decade would see some stunning creations.

Chiltern Babykins

Where to see Dolls in the UK

Dolls Museum, Memorial Hall, High Street, Dunster, Minehead, TA24 6SF

Lilliput Doll and Toy Museum, Brading, Isle of Wight, PO36 0DJ

Memories of Childhood, Ullapool, Kyleesku, Sutherland, 1V27 4HW

National Trust Museum of Childhood, Sudbury, Ashbourne, Derbyshire, DE6 5HT

Penrhyn Castle, Bangor, Gwynedd, LL57 4HN

Vina Cooke Museum of Dolls & Bygone Childhood, The Old Rectory, Great North Road, Cromwell, Newark, Nottinghamshire, NG23 6JE

V & A Museum of Childhood, Cambridge Heath Road, Bethnal Green, London, E2 9PA

Dolls' Hospitals

Bristol Doll and Teddybear Hospital, 1 Wycliffe Row, St Luke's Crescent, Bristol, BS3 4RU

Crafts Unlimited, 5 Scratton Road, Stanford le Hope, Essex, SS17 0NZ

Dolls Hospital, Beck House, Lower Street, Southrepps, Norwich, Norfolk, NR11 8UL

Dolly Doctors, The Doll Infirmary, 13 Windsor Road, Thanington Without, Kent, CT1 3UN

Day Dream Dolls, 142–144 Middlewich Road, Winsford, Cheshire, CW7 3NP

Recollect Dolls Hospital, 17 Junction Road, Burgess Hill, West Sussex, RH15 0HR

Teddy Bear Clinic & Dolls Hospital, The Dolls House, Stonehall Common, Kempsey, Worcester, Worcestershire, WR5 3QQ

Vina Cooke, The Old Rectory, Great North Road, Cromwell, Newark, Nottinghamshire, NG23 6JE

Further Reading

A LIST OF BOOKS RELATING TO 1960s' DOLLS OR DOLL COMPANIES:

British Teenage Dolls by Frances Baird, New Cavendish

British Toy Business by Kenneth D. Brown, Hambledon Press

Cleaning and Caring by Susan Brewer, Virtual Valley

Doll Showcase Looks At Amanda Jane by Susan Brewer, Virtual Valley

Pollock's Dictionary of English Dolls edited by Mary Hillier, Crown

Tiny Tears and First Love; Two Classic Baby Dolls by Susan Brewer, Virtual Valley

The Collector's Guide to British Dolls since 1920 by Colette Mansell, Hale

The Collector's Guide to British Teen Dolls by Colette Mansell, Mayberry Historical Publishing

The Peggy Nisbet Story by Peggy Nisbet, Hobby House Press

The Ultimate Doll Book by Caroline Goodfellow, Dorling Kindersley

The companion volume to this book is: *British Dolls of the 1950s* by Susan Brewer, Pen and Sword

Acknowledgements

There isn't room to list everyone who helped out with this book, but grateful thanks go to the following:

Lesley Glover, Aly Simmonds, Sally Tuffin, Marion Foale, Shelly Baxter, Doris Howe, Lee Beaumont, Shelley Cuff, Sharon White, Shirley Karaba, Audrey Robinson, Maggie Gustafson, Roberta Snape, Sue Wells, Jeanette Nott, Christine Poulten, Karen Conn, Anne McAndrew, Lorna Kaufman and Linda Clarke.

Special thanks go to my husband Malcolm for his support, son Simon for his technical help and daughter Jenna for the many hours she spent sorting and listing the dolls.

Picture Credits

Shelly Baxter 85, 86, 87
Linda Clarke 70
Marion Foale 54
Lesley Glover 103, 106, 129, 153, 181, 184, 198
Christine Poulten 160, 161, 162
Aly Simmonds 51, 52, 53, 55, 57, 58, 60, 62
Roberta Snape 133
Vectis 30, 66, 113, 117, 200, 201, 202 (upper)
William Warne 8, 171
Sharon White 186
Chris Wimsey 117, 125

Other illustrations belong to the author

Index